Simple. Direct. Relevant. Biblical. Ma.... ....
his preaching and his person. Anyone who reads this will
enjoy a return to the simple, great, and lofty presentation of the
old-time religion of the person of Jehovah. Mac will bless you.

  —Tommy Nelson, Senior Pastor,
   Denton Bible Church, Denton, Texas

My friend Mac Brunson understands the God-shaped vacuum
in our culture. The God You've Been Searching For *intro-*
duces us to the true God, and inspires us to get to know this
God in a personal way.

  —David Jeremiah, Senior Pastor, Shadow
   Mountain Community Church, and President,
   Turning Point Ministries, El Cajon, California

My friend Mac Brunson offers a powerfully clear and com-
pelling case for knowing, experiencing, and loving God. For a
culture confused in the fog of religious tolerance and political
correctness, Mac shows the way through using the penetrating
rays of biblical truth.

  —Joseph M. Stowell, author of *The Trouble*
   with Jesus, and Teaching Pastor,
   Harvest Bible Chapel

THE GOD
YOU'VE BEEN
SEARCHING FOR

MAC BRUNSON

MOODY PUBLISHERS
CHICAGO

Library of Congress Cataloging-in-Publication Data

Brunson, Mac, 1957-
    The God you've been searching for / Mac Brunson.
        p. cm.
    Includes bibliographical references.
    ISBN-13 0-8024-1373-4
    1. God—Biblical teaching. 2. Bible. O.T. Isaiah—Criticism,
interpretation, etc. I. Title.

BS1192.6.B78 2004
231—dc22

                                                2003020870

ISBN: 0-8024-1373-0
ISBN-13: 978-0-8024-1373-4

1 3 5 7 9 10 8 6 4 2

Printed in the United States of America

To my precious wife, Deb,
whose love, support, encouragement, and steadfastness
have enabled me to be more
than I could have ever been without her.

. . . and to Courtney, Trey, and Wills
who made our love complete
and our lives an adventure.

CONTENTS

FOREWORD

WHEN THE APOSTLE PAUL entered the city of Athens, Greece, he was astounded at the many idols. One historian estimates that there were more than 30,000 statues lining the streets of the city. Athens, the cultural center of Greece, was the home of altars, shrines, temples, and idols.

If Paul had been like many in our politically correct and culturally tolerant society, he would have praised the city for its diverse religious opportunities. But Luke tells us "his spirit was provoked within him when he saw that the city was given over to idols" (Acts 17:16).

Instead of being impressed, Paul was provoked. One of the strongest words in the New Testament is used to express his anguish of soul. He hated what he saw in Athens because it robbed the true God of His glory.

When Paul addressed the Athenians he said, "I perceive that in all things you are very religious" (Acts 17:22). He told them that they worshipped "an unknown god." What an apt description of the spiritual climate of our day. We are religious, yet we do not know God. Like Athens, we have multiplied our deities while pushing the real God into the background. We have reduced Almighty God to a topic of discussion when He longs to be the object of our worship.

My friend Mac Brunson understands the God-shaped vacuum in our culture. *The God You've Been Searching For* introduces us to the true God, the creator of the universe, the architect of redemption . . . the God of the Bible. And Pastor Brunson does not stop with an introduction to God . . . he does more than inform us. He inspires us to get to know this God in a personal way. He challenges us to embrace His love, accept His forgiveness, and acknowledge His abundant goodness.

I'm delighted that you've decided to read this book about God. If you have never known Him in a personal way, accept Him now—you will discover how in this book.

If you already know God but the relationship has grown cold, allow *The God You've Been Searching For* to rekindle that fire.

> Dr. David Jeremiah
> Senior Pastor,
> Shadow Mountain Community Church
> President, Turning Point Ministries

ACKNOWLEDGMENTS

NO BOOK, MINISTRY, OR LIFE is a solo work, but is a compilation of many sources. I would like to thank my parents, Don and Lil Brunson, for providing a wonderful home, a godly example, and deep devotion to the things of God. Their relationship with the Lord is real, both in public and behind closed doors. What I accomplish in life, I owe to the grace of God that placed me in their arms. In that home were two sisters, Donnie and Fran, who are as dear to me as sisters could possibly be.

I owe a deep debt of gratitude to the churches I have pastored:

First Damascus Baptist, Greenwood, SC.
South Norfolk Baptist, Chesapeake, VA
Green Street Baptist, High Point, NC

What wonderful congregations, who permitted me to be me, and allowed God to work through me. They have all been very patient, and encouraging.

And now to the great and historic congregation of the First Baptist Church of Dallas. This church is the closest thing to heaven on earth, where the saints are real, the faith is deep, and the Word of God is honored.

I want to say a special word of thanks to Deede Signoretto whose persistence, help, and encouragement really made this work possible.

In closing, let me say a word of appreciation to my editor at Moody Publishing, Mark Tobey, for his wonderful spirit and faithful counsel. To Tracy Sumner for his expertise, counsel, and persistence. His God-given gift is on every page of this book.

INTRODUCTION

SEVERAL YEARS AGO, someone asked theologian and philosopher R. C. Sproul, "What, in your opinion, is the greatest spiritual need in the world today?"

Without hesitation, Sproul replied, "The greatest need in people's lives today is to discover the true identity of God."

Then came this follow-up question: "What is the greatest spiritual need in the lives of church people?"

Again without hesitation, Sproul answered, "To discover the true identity of God. If believers really understood the character and the personality and the nature of God, it would revolutionize their lives."

I couldn't agree with Dr. Sproul's assessment more.

We live in a time of tremendous hunger for God, a time when millions are trying all sorts of religions and belief systems in order to find Him. People want more than a spiritual experience—they want something that makes a difference in their day-to-day lives.

This is true of the world around us. And it's true in our churches.

Does that surprise you? Does it seem strange that people who profess to be God's children often have trouble finding Him and feeling His reality, His presence? Or does this seem sadly close to your own experience?

Well, I'll let you in on a little secret: The truth is, many of us who are professing, Bible-believing Christians haven't been revolutionized by God's Good News in Jesus Christ. We struggle along, barely able to hold ourselves together in the face of life's everyday pressures, our inner temptations, and the world's opposition, let alone our enemy's attacks. Many of us feel powerless, impotent, and defeated in our spiritual lives.

As a fellow struggler, I've asked myself why that is. And here's what I think. I believe it's because we don't truly understand and know our God well enough. We don't comprehend the power He's made available to us to live joyful lives for Him, lives that bear real fruit for His kingdom. It's like we're people who walk into a darkened art gallery, unable to find the light switch—unable to enjoy the beauty around us.

In reality, I've discovered that it's actually wonderfully simple to find the light switch God has provided and illuminate our lives with His power through Jesus Christ. My goal in writing this book is to help us all

see that the God who wants to do this for us is the
God we've been searching for.

The Westminster Shorter Catechism of 1647 says
this same thing with a slight twist. Using a question-
and-answer format, it begins like this:

> Question: What is the chief and highest end of
> man?
> Answer: Man's chief and highest end is to glorify
>   God, and fully enjoy Him forever.

This tells us something wonderful about our reason for being. Most Christians understand that we
are here to glorify God, to serve Him with our lives in
such a way as to draw people's attention to Him and
His life-giving grace. But there is a very special "and"
in the answer to the question concerning our chief
end. It brings us to the second part of our calling: to
enjoy God.

Serving God is one thing, but *enjoying* Him? For
some of us, that may seem like a bit much to swal-
low. But it's the truth! This proclamation reflects these
blessed words of Jesus: "I came that they might have
life, and might have it *abundantly*" (John 10:10, emphasis added).

If there's one thing we all need to get through our
heads and into our hearts about the God we've been
searching for, it's this: He truly and deeply wants to
bless each of us with abundant life so that we might
actually *enjoy* Him now and into all of eternity.

We need to realize that God *wants* to bless us. He

wants us to know that He loves us and desires for us to know Him personally and intimately. He yearns for us to walk in His love and forgiveness and rest in knowing that He guides us and controls our futures.

Is this the God you've been searching for? If so, read on!

CHAPTER ONE

SEARCHING FOR THE SACRED

Thou has created us for thyself, and our hearts are restless until they rest in thee.

■ AUGUSTINE OF HIPPO

SEVERAL YEARS AGO, the magazine *Psychology Today* devoted a fascinating article and a full page of photographs to one of the country's most successful commodities traders, Philip John Neimark.

Neimark, the article pointed out, holds several honorary doctorates and is considered in many circles to be one of the sharpest businessmen in America. At the time of the article, he managed some $40 million in investments with an average return of 20 percent per year.

The article's focus, however, wasn't on Neimark's impressive business credentials but on his religion. He is a high priest of the ancient African religion Ifa. One photograph showed him dressed in his embroidered ceremonial robe in his converted garage, where he prays and makes animal sacrifices to the deity Orunmila.[1]

Personally, I was amazed that a man of such education and stature in the business world would be drawn toward this type of religion. This just didn't fit with my picture of people who were vulnerable to the influence of cults. But Philip John Neimark is obviously not one of the vulnerable. So, I wondered, what attracted him to this?

Despite his success and achievements, in reality he really isn't so different from the millions in our world who are dissatisfied with their careers, unfulfilled in their relationships, and disillusioned with their government and other institutions. Like the rest of us who so often struggle just to get through life, Neimark probably sensed that something was missing—something that power, success, and money couldn't provide.

I believe that Philip Neimark was searching for the sacred, but like so many others today—including many professing Christians—he was looking in profane places.

WHEN PROFANE REPLACES SACRED

Sigmund Freud once predicted that as humanity embraced science, we would lose interest in spiritual things. But I think that exactly the opposite has taken place. I believe that now, more than ever, people are looking for meaning in the spiritual. We may use phrases such as "trying to find myself" or "looking for meaning in life" or even "trying to find God." But when we get right down to it, we are looking for something sacred, something "set apart" that we can build and order our lives around.

Each of us has a hunger in our hearts for what is truly sacred—for a personal relationship with God. We have a God-created hole in each of our hearts that only our Creator can fill. And nothing else—not alternative religions, not science, not careers or possessions or relationships—can truly satisfy our hungry spirits. Truth be told, these often leave us more unfulfilled and needy than before.

But still we look for the sacred in profane places. Is this unique to our generation, our sped-up, industrialized century? No, it's a human tendency that runs throughout all of history. In the Old Testament book of Isaiah, we see exactly this kind of spiritual condition, even in God's own people.

Isaiah was a powerful prophet of God, one of the greatest in the history of Israel. For over sixty years, through the reigns of four kings, he confronted, comforted, and called the people of Judah to repentance. His was a time of national, international, political, personal, and spiritual crisis. God had warned him that his task would not be easy:

> "Go, and tell this people:
> 'Keep on listening, but do not perceive;
> Keep on looking, but do not understand.'
> Render the hearts of this people insensitive,
> Their ears dull,
> And their eyes dim.
> Otherwise they might see with their eyes,

Hear with their ears,
Understand with their hearts,
And repent and be healed." (Isaiah 6:9–10)

This is the tragic picture of a people God had greatly blessed but who were spiritually deaf, blind, and insensitive. They couldn't hear their heavenly Father when He spoke to them, and they couldn't see Him and the wonderful works He had done for them. They had filled themselves with idolatry, injustice, the pursuit of wealth, drunkenness, and illicit sexual pleasures.

I don't want to give you the impression that this was a hopeless situation. Far from it! In fact, in the midst of all this spiritual insensitivity, Isaiah had an overwhelmingly sacred encounter with God.

AT THE THRONE OF THE TRULY SACRED

I doubt that Isaiah could have prepared in any way for what would happen that day. He didn't go to the temple thinking he would actually see God or hear His voice—at least not in such a spectacular fashion. Isaiah was just doing what he had done countless times before: simply going to the temple to pray.

But he was about to have an encounter with the sacred like none he had ever had before. He stood at the doorway of the temple, looking through the outer court into the Holy Place. Then everything around him suddenly began to dissolve as the throne of God came into view. The base of the throne sat on the ground, and the top of it stretched toward the heavens. Smoke and fire filled the temple, six-winged heavenly beings called seraphim flew over the throne of God singing praises, and the whole temple began quaking at the sound of God's voice (see 6:1–4).

If you've ever endured a strong earthquake, you know that feeling of terror (although some of my friends in southern California claim they're used to it by now). It's as if the ground beneath you turns to quivering jelly, and your heart pounds as you realize you are completely helpless. Everything around you rocks and rolls, and there is nothing you can do and nowhere you can hide. You are truly at the mercy of nature's fury.

If you add to that kind of terror a vision of almighty God Himself on His throne, of unearthly beings singing His praises, of smoke and fire, and of God's thunderous voice, you can only begin to understand the awe and fear Isaiah surely felt that day.

Isaiah had a revelation of God as He is. "I saw the Lord sitting on a throne, lofty and exalted, with the train of His robe filling the temple" was all he could say (v. 1). This description of God's glory speaks of His sovereignty, His authority, His potency, and His overwhelming glory.

It's an awesome picture, but this is the kind of vision each of us searchers needs to hold of God. It's a view of what is truly sacred! And it's a vision we can have for ourselves if we but search in the right places with the right motivation.

I believe that the vast majority of Christians do things to "seek God," but we have no real idea why we are doing them. Many of us go to church on Sundays because that's what we do in our culture, because it's the Baptist, Presbyterian, Evangelical, or Church of Christ thing to do. We spend our time reading the Bible and praying because that is what "good Christians" do. We do these things because we were raised to do them, because we want to be better people, because we want to improve our marriages, because we want our children to have a good foundation for life.

Well, is this so wrong? Not at all. Desiring these things is healthy and right. But, and you knew a *but* was coming, they should never be our primary purpose for going to church, reading our Bibles, or praying. When we approach God with these things as our primary motivation, we actually walk away from our so-called spiritual experiences unchanged and without a revelation of the sacred.

Our desire and prayer, instead, should be to get a vision of God so overwhelming that we can do nothing but get on our faces before Him. When that happens, everything else will dissolve and the glory of the living God will come into view.

Let's take a moment to consider who and what Isaiah saw, how he responded to that vision, and what it means to us today.

First, there's the Lord's throne. That throne must be a wondrous and overwhelming sight, but that's not what we should be caught up in. Rather, our attention needs to be turned toward the beauty and splendor of the One who sits on that throne.

God's posture and position on His throne shows us some wonderful things about Him. It reveals His absolute authority, sovereignty, and potency. Our God, the One who is truly sacred, is ruler over everything and every other ruler. His rule is absolutely independent—He owes nothing to nor needs anything from anyone.

Isaiah 6 is an incredible picture of the awesomeness of our God. One morning, as I studied this passage, God spoke to my heart and showed me some things about Himself, about His throne, and about some things we will never have to worry about.

God Will Never Leave His Throne

Unlike earthly kings, who leave their thrones for love or more prosaic reasons such as political revolt, old age, or death, God will never abdicate His position on His throne. No one or no thing can ever take it from Him. He is the Lord both now and forever, and He will occupy His throne for all of eternity. We humans may choose to serve and worship other "gods," but the true and living God will remain on His throne, ruling heaven and earth.

You see, the Lord does not derive His power and authority from us. That's only true of the gods of our own hands and hearts. Do you remember the story of the prophet Elijah's contest against the prophets of Baal (see 1 Kings 18)? Each side was to make an altar and prepare a bull for the sacrifice—and then each would call on their respective deity. The one who answered by fire would be proven to be the true God. Being a gentleman as well as a prophet, Elijah let Baal's servants go first.

They built their altar, cut up their sacrifice, and called on their god. And called and called. All morning until noon. "O Baal, answer us!" But Baal said nothing. At the moment of their greatest need, their god was nowhere to be found.

Elijah, standing alone before these false prophets, laughed at them and at their god. The Scripture says,

> At noon Elijah began to taunt them. "Shout louder!" he said. "Surely he is a god! Perhaps he is deep in thought, or busy, or traveling. Maybe he is sleeping and must be awakened." (v. 27 NIV)

Baal's prophets grew frantic, shouted louder, and began cutting themselves until their blood streamed down. This awful spectacle went on until evening. "But there was no response, no one answered, no one paid attention" (v. 29 NIV).

That's what gods stamped with "Made on Earth" are capable of—nothing.

The one true Lord, however, is never away from His throne. He's never busy, asleep, or away on business. You'll never hear an angelic voicemail message saying, "I'm sorry. The Lord is out of the office until next week and can't be reached." He came through for Elijah and His people, showing them what the real God could do.

Elijah not only built an altar and dressed the sacrifice, he soaked everything three times with water until all was drenched. Then he called on the Lord and stood back. Whoosh! Fire streaked from heaven and licked up the sacrifice, the firewood, the altar stones, the water, and even the soil underneath and around it.

The God of Elijah's day is the same God of our day! And He isn't going anywhere. Though we may turn away from Him or get sidetracked, God remains on His throne, sovereignly ruling over everything.

Do you see, we can count on Him! He's a God who makes Himself available to those who seek Him.

Our God Is Always Available to Us

If there's one thing the gods of this world (both the material gods and the religious ones) all have in common it's this: They may give the seeker a temporary sense of fulfillment or happiness, but they will always display the character of false gods—arbitrary, up-and-down, uncaring, and unloving.

A god who behaves like that is no god at all, is it?

When we place false gods on the thrones of our hearts—including the gods of material wealth, success, power, or human relationships—we set ourselves up for a fall. That's because if we don't perform to certain standards, these gods will always fail us. Everything depends on us. And worse, in the end, we will always take on the character of the god we worship. That's a scary thought, isn't it?

Not so when we place the truly sacred, loving Creator on the throne of our hearts. Time and again God promises us, in both the Old and New Testaments, that He makes Himself available to us when we simply draw near to Him. We can rest assured that our God will never isolate Himself from us and that He'll never deny us the opportunity to approach Him.

The writer of the epistle to the Hebrews put it this way: "Let us draw near *with confidence* to the throne of grace, so that we may receive mercy and may find grace to help in time of need" (Hebrews 4:16, emphasis added).

When we are in a "time of need," when our worlds are shaken and things seem to be falling apart before our very eyes, we have a God who cares for us and desires that we approach Him *confidently* with hands open for His blessing. When we approach our relationship with Him as sacred, we can know beyond a doubt that He makes Himself available to us.

Knowing we can come close to almighty God that way, we can do only one thing in response: Praise His wonderful name!

Our God Is Worthy of Praise

Many of the things we put on the thrones of our hearts are, in and of themselves, good, enjoyable, and worth working for. For example, there is nothing wrong with working hard to build a successful career.

And no one can criticize us for doing the things necessary to improve our relationship with our spouse.
And we're likely to receive encouragement when we
try to build a strong life foundation for our children.

When put in the proper place, these things are
well worth our time and effort. But are they worthy of
our praise? Worthy to be worshiped and adored? Worthy to be treated as sacred? Not even close!

Only One is worthy of the kind of praise I'm talking about here. He's the One Isaiah saw for himself.
The One for whom the seraphim sang out their praise.

The seraphim are extraordinary creatures, more
bright and beautiful than anything we could ever
imagine. The Hebrew word for *seraphim* literally means
"fiery ones" or "burning ones," so we know they shine
brightly. They have faces, hands, feet, voices, and,
obviously, a sense of who God is. But what makes
them extraordinary isn't their appearance or their
voices—but their sole purpose for being.

They don't guard God's throne. That would be
like giving a five-year-old boy a peashooter to pro-
tect the 82nd Airborne. They also don't minister to
us, as other angelic beings do. Then what do they do?
Isaiah spells out God's purpose for them: "And one
called out to another and said, 'Holy, Holy, Holy, is
the LORD of hosts, The whole earth is full of His glory'"
(Isaiah 6:3). They are dedicated solely to praising God.

This is the only biblical passage that mentions
them by name, but others mention angelic beings
who praise God's name. In Daniel 7:10, for example,
we read of "thousands upon thousands" of spiritual

creatures whose job was to "attend Him"—in other words, to serve Him and give Him praise.

These passages bring us to this very important question: With literally thousands of heavenly creatures with nothing to do but lift up God's name, why should it matter to Him that we mere, frail humans offer Him words and deeds of praise? What could He really want to do with any of us? Why does He give each of us this eternally profound message: "I want you to praise My Name!"?

The answer is simple, yet wonderful. You see, God doesn't *force* us to praise Him. If He wanted to, He could compel us to speak words of praise and worship during our every waking hour. But He doesn't do that. He created us as those who could and would worship Him out of our own free will—*because we want to.*

God wants willing, joyous praise from those whom He made capable of enjoying a loving, personal relationship with Him. God created angelic beings who sing Him wonderful heavenly praises day and night, forever and ever. But to Him, there is no sweeter praise, no more lovely song of worship, than the one sung by those He has created and redeemed.

God doesn't *need* our praises. He doesn't need our approval or His ego stroked. Our words of praise don't make Him any greater or any more sure of who He is.

Why, then, does God want us to praise Him?

So He can bless us, that's why! So He can share Himself with us. So we can have a loving, personal relationship with Him. So He can allow us a glimpse of His awesome glory. When we open our mouths and our hearts to offer praises to our Father in heaven, we gain access to the very throne itself—and to the One who sits on that throne.

That is what the sacred looks like. That's the breathtaking picture of Himself that He wants each of us to capture.

Yes, we praise God because it brings us to a point where we can receive His blessings. But more than that, we do it because He is worthy. After all, He's God! And He's also the One who makes us worthy to speak the angels' language, His praises.

THE PROFANE MADE SACRED

When Isaiah saw this awesome vision and realized he was being drawn into the very presence of almighty God, his reaction was one of absolute awe and fear—even terror. The first words out of his mouth were, "Woe is me, for I am ruined!" (Isaiah 6:5). This word *woe* denotes horror, disaster, and judgment. Isaiah himself used this word at least ten times to describe God's judgment on others. So, when he said, "Woe is me!" he speaks judgment on himself.

Yet he was a righteous man of God, a prophet to God's own people. Why does he pronounce judgment on himself and tremble with such fear? He gives us the answer in his next words: "I am a man of unclean lips."

Unclean lips? On a prophet of God? How can that be?

When you think of this phrase, what comes to mind? Certainly speaking dishonestly or deceitfully. Profanity, cursing, swearing, and telling dirty stories all qualify. These things all come from "unclean lips," but Isaiah was not talking about anything like that.

I believe that he wanted to sing the same words that the myriads of angels did. But as he stood before the throne of God, he realized he wasn't worthy.

Isaiah understood something we all need to lay hold of—that the very best we have to offer, all our talents and skills and gifts, are profane before God. Remember, Isaiah was a prophet, and the most valuable tool he had was his mouth—the mouth that spoke the prophecies of God. But he knew that his mouth was unclean, that it wasn't good enough to speak to God. Standing in this awesome scene of God's power and greatness, he realized he was a sinner, that the best part of him was profane—and it literally left him speechless.

What do you think happened next? Did God destroy him? Did He crush the prophet? Did He send him out of His presence for all of eternity? No! Instead of turning this profane man back into dust, the Lord lovingly took the initiative and made Isaiah worthy to stand in His presence and speak praises to Him.

The Bible tells us that one of the seraphim went to the altar, took a live, hot coal, then touched it to Isaiah's lips and pronounced him clean before God: "Behold, this has touched your lips; and your iniquity is taken away, and your sin is forgiven" (v. 7).

God Himself made the provision for His servant,

removing the barrier of sin so He could draw Isaiah near.

THE SACRED MADE ACCESSIBLE

Being in the presence of almighty God is certainly an awesome and breathtaking experience—even for a man of God like Isaiah. But God shows us in this passage that His awesome presence is for our benefit and blessing. He alone provides us with the worthiness to approach Him and stand before His throne.

This soul-wrenching picture of God's glory is also a marvelous picture of His love, forgiveness, and redemption. God provided what none of us could provide for ourselves: righteousness, cleansing, and worthiness. Now we can actually approach God's throne knowing that we are loved and welcomed with open, compassionate arms.

Isaiah had a chance to see firsthand what all men and women are looking for right now: the truly sacred. He was allowed to stand in the presence of the true and living God, to communicate face-to-face with the One who made the way for him to fellowship with Him in all His glory.

Now here's the wonderful Good News: God has done the same thing for each and every one of us. We live in the age of the New Covenant, when we can approach Him and truly enjoy life in the sacred. And He's done so much more for us than send an angel— a created being—to purify our lips with a burning coal. He's sent His very own Son. Jesus Christ gave

Himself on the Cross so that not just our lips can be purified but our entire being.

This brings us to why most people's search for the sacred comes up short. When we look for the sacred in any place other than in the person of the true and living God, we are sure to find ourselves disappointed, unfulfilled, and, ultimately, lost. Every other path we may choose in our search for the sacred has us taking the initiative, has us doing the things we believe will fulfill us and give us life.

But it's different with God.

Each of us who searches for the sacred needs to know that *God has taken the initiative.* He has taken the steps to make things right between Himself and us—to cleanse us, forgive us, and save us. It is through Jesus' work on the Cross of Calvary that God sends us this blessed message: "I love you and I forgive you! Come near to Me!"

None of us needs to search for the sacred any longer, because the sacred took the initiative to come looking for us—in the person of Jesus Christ. It is through what He did on the Cross that we can have true fulfillment through a relationship with the Creator God.

Knowing this, we can rest assured that our search for the sacred ends in one place and one place only: at the foot of the Cross!

REFLECTIONS FOR
INDIVIDUAL OR SMALL GROUP STUDY

1. In what ways do you see people today searching for the sacred?

2. Why do people today posses such strong desires to explore their spirituality?

3. How have 9/11 and events since contributed to an increased interest in spiritual things?

4. In what ways has the church been successful in answering seekers' questions? Unsuccessful?

5. How did this look at Isaiah 6 help you?

6. How might these truths help a seeker?

CHAPTER TWO

THE GOD YOU CAN KNOW

Knowledge of God can be fully given to man only in a Person, never in a doctrine. Faith is not the holding of correct doctrine, but personal fellowship with the living God.

■ WILLIAM TEMPLE

CHARLES AND JOHN GREW UP in a devoutly religious home. Their father held a high position in the family church, and they attended meetings regularly. Both Charles and John received all the religious training two boys could possibly need. They attended Christian prep schools; then in college they took turns leading a group of men—a group Charles started—devoted to daily private prayer, Bible study, and discipleship. Eventually, John became an ordained minister.

The brothers wanted to do their part to fulfill the Great Commission—to make disciples worldwide—and they traveled together overseas to work as missionaries among "wayward," or unchurched, people. But their efforts to convert these souls led to nothing but frustration. There were few conversions, if any at all. It seemed to the brothers that they were wasting their time and God's with these people. After three years of nearly fruitless preaching and teaching, they decided to head back home to regroup.

Once home, these aspiring evangelists met a man named Peter, who talked to them about the Christian faith and what it meant to him personally. This conversation made a huge impression on both Charles and John. They knew that Peter had something they didn't. But what? What did these young men need to add to their lives?

Not long after that, Charles, who was recovering from an illness, had a chance to take stock of his own spiritual life. He realized what was missing, and on that Sunday afternoon in spring, for the first time Charles personally met the God he believed he had been serving his whole life. Three days later, at a church meeting he wasn't particularly thrilled to be attending, John followed his brother in placing his faith in Jesus Christ.

Does it surprise you to hear that two men who had devoted years to serving God could come to a point where they realized they didn't even know Him? Well, I can assure you this is a true story. You see, the people John and Charles had tried their hand at converting lived in an American colony called Georgia. And the home they returned to was England. This all took place over the first four decades of the eighteenth century.

I'm talking about Charles and John Wesley, two of the most influential and accomplished figures in the history of the Western church—John as a powerful preacher and evangelist, and Charles as a preacher and, more notably, the writer of many of the most beautiful hymns of praise and worship we have the privilege of singing.

Imagine that! Two of the most important men in the history of the European and American church came within a gnat's breath of missing out on God's kingdom altogether! And why? Because they had become so caught up in *doing* the things they believed pleased God that they neglected to get to know Him *personally*.

From the time they were small children, Charles and John Wesley knew *about* God. They had spent their youth studying the Bible and learning about discipleship and all other aspects of the Christian faith. Their heads were full of wonderful knowledge, but their hearts didn't really *know* God.

Their story points out something each of us needs to understand—that serving God and knowing about Him is not the same thing as knowing Him personally. And more than anything else, it is absolutely essential for us to know God that way.

KNOWING GOD VS. KNOWING *ABOUT* GOD

Jesus sternly underscored how crucial it is to know God personally. In His Sermon on the Mount, He spoke of the fate of those who based their salvation on seemingly righteous words and deeds but who lacked a personal relationship of faith and true obedience:

"Not everyone who says to Me, 'Lord, Lord,' will enter the kingdom of heaven; but he who does the will of My Father who is in heaven. Many will say to Me on that day, 'Lord, Lord, did we not prophesy in Your name, and in Your name cast out demons, and in Your name perform many miracles?' And then I will declare to them, 'I never knew you; DEPART FROM ME.'" (Matthew 7:21–23)

These might sound like harsh words coming from our Savior, but the point of Jesus' message is simple and clear: "If you want life eternal, you have to know Me!"

Each of us needs to answer one vital question: Do I really know God, or do I just know *about* Him?

The first key to really knowing God on a personal basis is knowing what He has said about Himself, rather than mastering what others have said about Him. We need to know what He has revealed about His thoughts, emotions, personality, and character.

To get an accurate picture of who God is, we need to turn to His written Word, the Bible. Here, in the book of Isaiah, we'll find one of many passages in which God tells us very specifically who He is and what it means to really know Him.

WHO DOES GOD SAY HE IS?

In Isaiah 44, God shows the people four wonderful things He wants them to know about Himself, four things which those who truly want to know Him will understand: "Thus says the LORD, the *King* of Israel And his *Redeemer*, the LORD *of hosts:* 'I am the first and I am the last, And there is no *God* besides Me'" (v. 6, emphasis added).

In one beautiful verse, we see God identifying Himself to us with four names: King, Redeemer, the Lord of hosts, and God. This is God speaking and telling us who He is.

Knowing Our God as King

As a minister, I've performed more weddings than I can count—so many, in fact, that I've memorized the basic vows by heart. One of those vows has to do with the husband and wife keeping themselves only for one another. This is a solemn promise that means no sharing, no "stepping out," and no taking time off to check out other options.

It means, as the last line of the vow goes, "For as long as you both shall live."

This is an earthly picture of the kind of commitment God wants from those who know Him. And it is what He means when He calls Himself King through the prophet Isaiah—seven centuries before the birth of the King of Kings, Jesus Christ.

The kingdom of Judah, to which Isaiah ministered, had wallowed in idolatry. But here is the paradox: They did not exactly turn *away* in disbelief from the God of Abraham, Isaac, and Jacob. They did not completely stop worshiping Him. Rather, they incorporated the gods of the nations around them into their worship.

This is spiritual infidelity, and it's something God takes very seriously. As He told the children of Israel: "For you shall not worship any other god, for the LORD, whose name is Jealous, is a jealous God" (Exodus 34:14). In other words, God says, "You are my people, and I love you. For that reason, I will not share your affections with anyone!"

This jealousy does not spring from any self-interest or ego, but it comes out of God's love for His people and His desire that they keep themselves true to Him—just as He has stayed true to them. It's a jealousy very much like the one my wife and I share, one built not on distrust and suspicion, which is how human jealousy usually works, but out of commitment to one another. We love one another so deeply and completely that we cannot and will not share our affections with another.

When we look at the love and commitment God pours out to His people—and we who know Jesus Christ are His people—it might seem hard to imagine us sharing ourselves with other gods. But we do that, don't we? And sometimes with a little help from our worst enemy.

Getting us to open up to other gods is one of Satan's most successful strategies. Our enemy is the master of deception. He wants to block us from knowing our God in an intimate way, and he'll use any means at his disposal to accomplish that goal. Satan usually doesn't put literal idols in our way; rather, he uses things that, when put in their proper places, can actually glorify God.

For example, if we make things such as comfort or success our idols or kings, or when we put success on the throne that God alone should occupy, we keep ourselves from truly knowing Him as deeply as He desires. And worse, when we embrace the world's illusions, we close our hearts to the God who is real. This will always keep us from knowing God, because He will never share the throne of our hearts with other gods.

If you want to know God—*really* know God personally—then you need to climb something that reaches infinitely higher than the ladder of success, and that is Mount Calvary. That is where you can kneel at the cross and see and know for yourself the God who is your very own King and Redeemer.

Knowing Our God as Redeemer

As Redeemer, God has done more than just cover over the stain of our sin so that it fades into the background. He completely removes that stain, using the blood of His Son, Jesus Christ, and then leaves behind something infinitely more beautiful. As He spoke through Isaiah, "I have wiped out your transgressions like a thick cloud, And your sins like a heavy mist. Return to Me, for I have *redeemed* you" (Isaiah 44:22, emphasis added).

In this context, the word *transgressions* is one of the strongest terms the Bible uses for sin. It literally means to "sin with a high hand" or to commit premeditated sin. This is open rebellion—doing what is wrong when we know what is right in God's sight.

But just as a good wind from the north can sweep even the most ominous-looking thunderclouds away, sparing us from the onslaught, so does God sweep away the clouds of sin that hang over our heads. This is the redemption of God, which He completed at the Cross of Calvary, the redemption each of us needs and receives when we know Him personally.

Knowing God as Lord

If I attempted to draw a picture of God, I'd want to make sure He was a God who is in control of my life as well as everything that goes on in the world. Is this who you would want to picture too? This would be a portrait of God as Lord.

Isaiah calls God "Lord of hosts," or as some translations put it "Lord Almighty." That's an awesome word picture, isn't it? Thinking of our God as the Almighty can be a little frightening. But when we remember that He is not only all-powerful but all-loving, this picture instills confidence, not fear.

The Lord challenges any and all comers to step up and prove that anyone or anything can compare with Him:

"'I am the first and I am the last,
And there is no God besides Me.

Who is like Me? Let him proclaim and
    declare it;
Yes, let him recount it to Me in order,
From the time that I established the ancient
    nation.
And let them declare to them the things that
    are coming
And the events that are going to take place.' "
(Isaiah 44:6–7)

That is God's proclamation of who He really is.
He is the One who created all, who sustains all, and
who brings all events to pass in a way that testifies to
His being in complete control.

When we know God as Lord, we can have an inde-
scribable peace because of the confidence we have in
Him. We know God personally, and we believe Him
when He tells us, "Do not fear, nor be afraid; Have I
not told you from that time, and declared it? You are
My witnesses. Is there a God besides Me? Indeed there
is no other Rock; I know not one" (v. 8 NKJV).

When we know God as Lord, we know that He is
the One we can turn to when we have no one else,
the One we can talk to when no one else will listen,
the One we can lean on when no one else stays close
by, the One we can depend on when all others fail us.

If you know God, you know Him as the God who
is Lord. You don't just know about *a* God who is in
control of everything, but you personally know *the*
God who is in control of your very own life.

Knowing Him as God

The fourth name God calls Himself is simply "God." In the original Hebrew, it is the name *Elohim*, and it is used more than two thousand times in Scripture, including in the very first verse in the Bible. This name identifies Him as the strong and mighty One, as the Creator who had the strength and power to call everything into existence—by nothing more than His own word.

God *created* the literally hundreds of billions of stars in our little section of the cosmos called the Milky Way. He *created* the billions of galaxies that comprise our universe. He *created* this earth and every living thing that inhabits it—from the smallest single-cell creatures to the largest mammals, reptiles, fish, and birds that walk the land, swim the seas, or fly in the air.

God didn't spare on the details when He created, either. He even went so far as to include in the head of the woodpecker a piece of padding so that this bird wouldn't beat its brain out when it pecked a hole in the bark of a tree looking for food. He gave certain fish the ability to take oxygen from the air when the water they live in becomes depleted during drier times. And He also took the time to design the human body, using seventy-five thousand miles and more of veins and arteries to supply literally tens of trillions (a trillion is a million million) of cells with oxygen- and nutrient-rich blood.

Yes, this is the God we've been searching for—the

God we can know personally—who created and designed *all* these things. But here's the really amazing part: God didn't need anyone's help to do it. And why? Because He and He alone is God!

Isaiah tells us that the God we can know—our King, Redeemer, and Lord—is the one and only God we can credit for all of creation: "Thus says the LORD, your Redeemer, and the one who formed you from the womb, 'I, the LORD, am the maker of all things, Stretching out the heavens by Myself, And spreading out the earth all alone'" (Isaiah 44:24).

This verse speaks of the magnificence of the Creator God, but it also carries the idea of covenant— specifically a love promise between the Maker and the ones He made. God wants us to know Him as the Creator, and He wants that knowledge to be of the personal, intimate kind.

That's the wondrous, unfathomable truth about the God we've been searching for: He took the time to create everything from the cosmos down to the tiniest life form, and yet it's important to Him that we know Him personally!

God wants us to have a personal relationship with Him, and He's placed only one condition on that personal knowledge: We have to want to know Him.

OUR PART IN THE BARGAIN: DESIRING TO KNOW HIM

Do you desire to know the God you've been reading about—*really* know Him? Are you merely curious about all this talk of a personal relationship with God, or do you have a passion to know Him? If so, I have great news. You see, God tells us over and over that a relationship with Him is possible if we do but one thing: seek and ask.

If you want to know how much God loves you and wants you to know Him, you need only read your Bible. The Word of God is a detailed account of our God—of His works, character, and heart of love for us. And it's also a personal invitation to each of us to draw near to Him and truly know Him.

Both the Old and New Testaments are chock-full of God's open invitation and encouragement to seek to know Him. Here are but a few examples:

> "But from there you will seek the LORD your God, and you will find Him if you search for Him with all your heart and all your soul." (Deuteronomy 4:29)

> "I love those who love me; And those who diligently seek me will find me." (Proverbs 8:17)

> "'Then you will call upon Me and come and pray to Me, and I will listen to you. And you will seek Me and find Me, when you search for me with all your heart.'" (Jeremiah 29:12–13)

> "Seek first His kingdom and His righteousness." (Matthew 6:33)

"Ask, and it shall be given to you; seek, and you shall find; knock, and it shall be opened to you. For everyone who asks receives, and he who seeks finds, and to him who knocks it shall be opened." (Matthew 7:7-8)

"Keep seeking the things above, where Christ is, seated at the right hand of God." (Colossians 3:1)

Jesus gave one final invitation to come to Him and know Him in a personal way: "'Behold, I stand at the door and knock; if any one hears My voice and opens the door, I will come in to him, and will dine with him, and he with Me'" (Revelation 3:20).

Consider those words for a moment. This is the Lord Jesus Christ, the very Son of God—our King, our Redeemer, our Lord, and our Creator—telling us He wants to come and dine with us, that He wants a warm, loving friendship with us lowly human beings.

This is the ultimate promise for those who seek to really know God. It tells us that when we hear His invitation, when we hear that knock at the door of our hearts, we can answer and enjoy a wonderful, eternal relationship with our King, our Redeemer, our Lord, our God.

That is God's desire for you personally. And if you share that desire, then He's the God you've been searching for.

REFLECTIONS FOR
INDIVIDUAL OR SMALL GROUP STUDY

1. What is the difference between knowing about God and truly knowing God? What Scripture passages help make this distinction?

2. How did you respond to the biblical notion that God is jealous for you and for your affection?

3. In what ways has God revealed Himself in the Bible as "Redeemer"? "Lord"? "Creator"?

4. How has God revealed Himself to you?

5. Why do you think there is such confusion about who God really is?

6. What are some ways you and the church you are part of can make God known?

CHAPTER THREE

THE BRIDGE GOD BUILT

Ah! The bridge of grace will bear your weight, brother. Thousands of big sinners have gone across that bridge, yea, tens of thousands have gone over it. . . . I will go with them trusting to the same support; it will bear me over as it has borne them.

■ CHARLES SPURGEON

THE LACEY V. MURROW BRIDGE—also known as the Lake Washington Floating Bridge—stretches over the lake from the Mount Baker neighborhood of Seattle, Washington, to the north end of Mercer Island. It was, for its time, an engineering and design marvel.

In the late 1930s, there was a real need for a bridge over Lake Washington. The population of the area was growing rapidly, and commuters needed a quicker way to cross from Seattle to Mercer Island. But bridge designers and builders were faced with some engineering problems. First of all, this bridge was to span over water that was up to two hundred feet deep. Second, the bottom of the lake in many spots was nothing but soft mud, meaning that the bridge pilings would most likely sink into the earth and disappear.

Obviously, it would not be possible to build a conventional bridge over that part of Lake Washington. So engineer Homer Hadley designed the world's first floating bridge, an amazing innovation. It was 6,620 feet long and held up by twenty-two hollow concrete pontoons, each 350 feet long by 59 feet wide by 14 feet deep. Holding the pontoons in place were cables attached to 65-ton anchors that were held together end-to-end by four-inch solid rubber gaskets.

The Lake Washington Floating Bridge was designed with one problem in mind—that no ordinary bridge could span the gulf of Lake Washington. As amazing as it was, however, it wasn't nearly as amazing as what God did to bridge the gulf between Himself and a lost humanity.

The bridge God built spanned something infinitely deeper and wider than Lake Washington. It was made not out of concrete, steel, cables, and asphalt but out of two pieces of wood and the blood of His very own Son, Jesus Christ.

A MAN-MADE GULF

Have you ever endured the heartache of a completely severed relationship? Maybe you couldn't—or wouldn't—forgive a one-time close friend for some wrongdoing, or a friend refused to forgive you. Either way, the relationship was destroyed, and it broke your heart.

This is just what happened to humanity's relationship with God. We are all in a place where our fellowship with Him has been severed. Yet God never intended it to be this way.

Maybe you're like me. Sometimes, when I look at myself and the life I've lived—especially the things I so desperately wish I could change—I find it difficult to believe that God created *me* for the purpose of having perfect, uninterrupted, unimpeded fellowship for all of eternity. Well, it's true for me and for you!

God created us for the very purpose of having fellowship with Himself. I'm talking about an intimate, close relationship, one where sinless human beings can look God right in the face—like a best friend, without fear or guilt. The Bible tells us in Genesis that after God finished creating the universe and the earth it contains, after He created all living creatures, including the only one He could have fellowship with, He actually walked in the garden with the man and woman.

But something tragic took place that would change that relationship for the rest of human history.

One day, as God walked through the garden, He called out to Adam and Eve, "Where are you?" From behind some bushes, a terrified and suddenly self-conscious man answered God, "I heard the sound of You in the garden, and I was afraid because I was naked; so I hid myself" (Genesis 3:10).

I was afraid . . .

The man had never hidden from God before, had never been afraid to be in His presence. And until now, he never realized he was naked, either. He had spent hours and hours with God, with no self-consciousness about the body God had created.

Something happened. But what? What had fractured a perfectly harmonious relationship? What caused the man to shrink in fear from the God whose company prior to that day had meant nothing but comfort and security?

The answer to that is found earlier in Genesis 3, where we read of humanity's first act of rebellion.

God had created the man and then given him free reign of the garden, telling him that he could eat anything that looked good—with one exception: he must not eat from the tree of the knowledge of good and evil. If he did, he would "surely die" (2:16–17).

Adam and Eve had it all! A perfect relationship with one another and with their God and a beautiful garden to live in. There was just one simple command they needed to follow in order to keep all of this for eternity—"Don't eat from this one tree!"

But an enemy in snake's clothing approached the woman and began putting questions in her mind: "Did God really say you shall not eat from that tree? C'mon, He's holding out on you! Go ahead and eat . . . if you do, your eyes will finally be opened!" Satan was right about one thing: Her eyes *were* opened. But what he left out were the consequences of her actions.

The woman did as the devil suggested and then persuaded her husband to do the same. With that, sin and death came into the picture.

God would not be God if He didn't hold true to His word, and as He had warned the man, there were severe consequences if he should walk into disobedience. The man and the woman chose to disobey, and with eternally dreadful consequences. People would no longer live in perfect harmony with God, with their spouses, with their children, and with their world.

Because God is holy and cannot associate Himself with sin, He had to drive Adam and Eve out of the pristine beauty of the garden. The once-perfect fellowship between God and His people was broken—not just fractured, damaged, or amiss—but completely destroyed.

We must understand that God was not the One who broke the fellowship. I believe it broke God's heart to have to turn the crowning jewel of His creation—humankind—out of the garden. When Adam and Eve gave in to temptation, they chose rebellion and sin and in effect drove God out of their hearts. The good news in all this, however, is that humanity was not driven out of God's heart.

Humanity created an eternity-wide gulf of sin and rebellion, something we can do nothing to span in our own effort. But there is One who can do and wants to do something about it: God Himself.

A GOD-BUILT BRIDGE

Now, as you've probably seen or experienced, we still try to build all kinds of bridges or launch all kinds of boats in an attempt to cross that eternal gulf. But we end up feeling adrift, even hopeless. Deep within the soul of every one of us is the almost instinctive realization that we need to know God and be saved. But the question remains, How can we get to God from where we are now? How do we put that bridge in place?

The plain truth is, we can't. There is nothing we can do, no religion we can practice, no good works we can take part in to bring us any closer to the Lord.

But God has built that bridge between His heart and ours!

Let's take a look at the design and construction of the most wondrous bridge in all of history. The prophet Isaiah gives us a glimpse of the blueprint: "For thus says the high and exalted One Who lives forever, whose name is Holy, 'I dwell on a high and holy place, And also with the contrite and lowly of spirit In order to revive the spirit of the lowly And to revive the heart of the contrite'" (Isaiah 57:15).

This verse starts out by telling us some things about the God we have been searching for, but who we have been separated from because of our sin. And it tells us that He is like nothing we have ever imagined.

The Otherness of God

I don't believe it is possible using human words to adequately describe who and what our God is. But Isaiah gives us a small glimpse as to why we lowly human beings have been separated from Him. The prophet shows us that there is something vastly and eternally different about this God.

He is the high and exalted One. There is something about our fallen human nature that makes us want to drag things down to our level. We don't seem to like or

appreciate the idea of something— or someone—
being above us, or "up there."

We do that with some of God's greatest gifts to
humanity. We've certainly done that with human sexuality, haven't we? God intended our sexuality to be
used as a pleasurable expression of love between a
man and a woman within the security of a lifetime
commitment. But we've reduced it to, at best, mere
recreation and, at worst, smut and filth.

It's amazing and sad what we do with some of
God's finest gifts, isn't it? Even more awful, however,
is that we try to do that to God Himself.

Steven J. Lawson, in his book *Made in Our Image:
What Shall We Do with a "User-Friendly" God?*, wrote:
"In one way or another, we all attempt to reduce God
to humanlike dimensions based on what we can log-
ically understand by our limited thinking. We are all
tempted to think of Him on our level."[1]

Isaiah, however, gives a bracing antidote to our
tendency to demean the Lord. He tells us that our
God is high and exalted, meaning that He is above
everyone and everything else. No one can challenge
Him or compete with Him. He is exalted above every
throne, every ruler, every king, every monarch.

It's only possible for us to ever come close to Him
because He has taken the initiative to bridge the gulf
between Himself and us.

He is the eternal One. We have a difficult time
grasping eternity, being the mortal creatures that we
are. But this is exactly the realm in which the God we
serve and love lives. God exists outside the restraints

and constraints of time. In eternity past He always
was, and in eternity future He always will be. Jesus
said, "I am the Alpha and the Omega" (Revelation
1:8, 21:6, 22:13), meaning nothing was before Him
and nothing will be after Him.

He is the holy One. Isaiah recognized that God is
high and lifted up and that He is eternal, but he also
praises the one attribute of God that creates the need
for the bridge to Him we've been talking about. That's
His holiness.

God's holiness is a powerful theme running
throughout the Bible, especially in the book of Isaiah.
By my count, Isaiah uses the phrase "holy One" at
least twenty-seven times. It's as if he repeats that
phrase like a chorus of praise, as if he wants to pound
it into the minds of his people.

If you take your dictionary and look up the word
holy, you will see it defined as having to do with the
divine or with God, as having high spiritual or moral
worth. These are not *wrong* definitions, but they are
incomplete. Holy, as the Bible uses it in reference to
our God, suggests one who is set apart or separated.
When Isaiah uses that word to describe his God, he is
in effect saying that the Lord is the *one true holy God!*
This echoes some of the words of Moses: "Who is like
You among the gods, O LORD? Who is like You, majestic in holiness, Awesome in praises, working wonders?" (Exodus 15:11)

There is none like our God—in character, in
thought, in word, and in deed. He is the only One
who is absolutely perfect and flawless in every way. He

has never sinned, never will sin, cannot be tempted to sin, won't cause someone to sin, and cannot be in the presence of sin.

This is the God Isaiah praises. The God of absolute holiness.

This picture of God should be enough to frighten any of us sinful human beings. But thank God that's not all He tells us about Himself!

Yes, Isaiah tells us, God is an absolutely and perfectly holy God. But He's also a God who wants more than anything to identify with His people.

The God Who Identifies with Us

Yes, Isaiah tells us that God dwells in a high place set apart for Him alone. But the prophet also says that this high and holy God, the One who is eternal and above everything, has built a bridge from Himself to two kinds of people: the "contrite" and the "lowly of spirit" (Isaiah 57:15). David echoed that thought when he prayed, "The sacrifices of God are a broken spirit; A broken and a contrite heart, O God, You will not despise" (Psalm 51:17).

This really goes against some of the debased human pictures of God, doesn't it? It tells us that the "out there" god is gone, replaced by the God who wants to spend His time with those of us who need Him most. It says that the "performance first" god is dead, and in its place is the true and living God, who knows that apart from Him, we have nothing to offer.

Nowhere in the Bible do we find the message that

God dwells with the high and mighty, with the proud and self-sufficient. Nowhere does it tell us that God loves the "beautiful" people or the ones with the most talent and wealth to share with Him. On the contrary, in passage after passage, God conveys this message: "I resist the proud but give grace to the contrite and lowly in spirit."

He identifies with the contrite. The word *contrite*, as Isaiah uses it, literally means crushed to the point of being like powder. It means to crumble, as an old plaster wall crumbles into powder under the touch of a human hand. In His mercy and tenderness, God has built a bridge to those who are crushed by life and by the weight of their own sin—particularly those who *know* they are sinners in need of cleansing and forgiveness.

In the Gospel of Luke, chapter 18, Jesus presented a parable that demonstrates how God views the contrite. He told the story of two men—a Pharisee and a tax-gatherer—who went to a temple to pray.

To fully understand the point of this parable, you have to keep in mind that the Pharisee was a religious authority of the day. He knew the Law of Moses, as well as all the Jewish traditions—and he followed them *to the letter.* The tax-gatherer, on the other hand, was the ultimate in sinners. To call a tax-gatherer a scoundrel was to show great disrespect to self-respecting scoundrels.

When the Pharisee prayed, he thanked God that he was a just and righteous man, that he wasn't like others—and especially not like that miserable tax-gatherer over there! After all, he paid his tithes and fasted twice a week. He did everything he believed God required of him. "Lord," the Pharisee prayed, "I think I'm doing all right!" (vv. 11–12).

In the other corner of the temple was a man beaten down by the weight of his own sin, a man who knew of his own unworthiness, who knew how miserable he really was. He couldn't even look up toward heaven; rather, he just prayed over and over: "God, have mercy on me! I'm a sinner!" (v. 13).

Guess which one of these men Jesus said left the temple justified before God? If you guessed that it was that religious, self-righteous Pharisee, guess again! It was the tax-gatherer, the one who was contrite and humble before God about his own sinfulness.

Jesus created a stir among the religious authorities of the day by associating Himself with the kind of "sinners" He spoke of in this parable. He remarked on their view of Him: "The Son of Man came eating and drinking, and they say, 'Behold, a gluttonous man and a drunkard, a friend of tax-gatherers and sinners!'" (Matthew 11:19).

The Son of God demonstrated the love of His Father in that He didn't waste His time with those who thought they were righteous before Him. Rather, He spent His time with those who knew of their need for Him: sinners.

And I am overwhelmed with joy to tell you that to this day, nothing about Him has changed!

He identifies with the lowly of spirit. No one is closer to understanding what God has to offer than the one who realizes he or she has nothing to offer in return. These are the people God talked about through Isaiah when He referred to the "lowly of spirit."

We have a tendency to put ourselves down, to say things that make us seem humble and lowly in spirit, thinking God will honor us for that attitude. But that is not the "lowliness of spirit" God talks about. Lowliness of spirit means seeing ourselves honestly, seeing ourselves as wretched, miserable creatures who have nothing to offer God but outstretched, empty hands—hands that need to be filled with His goodness and righteousness.

I realize that this is not a popular view in some Christian circles. There is a brand of Christianity today that says it is unhealthy for us to think of ourselves as sinners. The great reformers such as Martin Luther, Ulrich Zwingli, John Knox, and the others did not think this way, nor did the "Pre-Reformation" reformers such as John Huss. The great preachers of history, such as Charles Simeon, John Newton, Charles Wesley, George Whitefield, D. L. Moody, Charles Spurgeon, and a host of others recognized that all of us are sinners. But much of contemporary Christianity has been diluted by pop psychology and infiltrated by a self-centeredness that rejects the idea of our fallen nature.

In contrast, Isaiah stood before God's throne and immediately realized how little he had to offer the Lord (Isaiah 6). He cried out, "Woe is me!" as the awesomeness of God's glory surrounded him. Isaiah showed the same "poorness of spirit" each of us needs to demonstrate if we are to find that bridge from God to us.

Isaiah tells us that God desires to "revive the spirit of the lowly And to revive the heart of the contrite" (57:15). To *revive* means to make alive again, to renew, and to quicken and nourish. When we cross the bridge to God, He gives us life! And not only that, He continues to nourish that life so that it can grow and flourish.

King David wrote of the compassion behind God's reaching out to those who are contrite and lowly of spirit: "The LORD is compassionate and gracious, Slow to anger and abounding in lovingkindness. He will not always strive with us; Nor will He keep His anger forever" (Psalm 103:8–9).

That, friends, is why our God—the high and holy God who designed and constructed everything around us—took the time to build that bridge from His heart to ours.

THE MOST EXPENSIVE BRIDGE EVER BUILT

I did some research about bridges, and I found out something that's true of every major bridge in the world: They're expensive!

The Salazar bridge in Lisbon, Portugal, cost $75 million to build, and the Walt Whitman bridge in Gloucester City, New Jersey, ran $90 million. The Virranzano Narrows Bridge in Brooklyn, New York, was built at a cost of $325 million. The most expensive bridge I found is the Seto-Ohashi Bridge in Shikoku, Japan, built at the mind-bending cost of $8.3 billion.

But the cost of all the world's bridges combined is nothing compared with the price God paid for the bridge from His heart to ours. That bridge cost Him *everything.* It cost Him His very own Son! The apostle Paul tells us that it was the Father's own choice to build this bridge: "He who did not spare His own Son, but delivered Him over for us all . . ." (Romans 8:32).

This is a picture of the most selfless, most generous act in all of history. Our heavenly Father, who had enjoyed perfect fellowship with His Son for all of eternity past, sent Him to die for us. At a key point in the horrible, heartrending, and, yes, *wonderful* scene of the crucifixion, Jesus looked to heaven, and with sheer terror and unimaginable pain in His heart, cried out "'Eloi, Eloi, lama sabachthani?' which is translated, 'My God, My God, why have You forsaken Me?'" (Mark 15:34). For the first time ever, the Father couldn't look at His own Son. Why? Because the Father had sent His Son to *become* sin for us, knowing He would have to turn His back on Him because He couldn't look upon sin.

Thankfully, that wasn't the end of the story. Far from it! When the sacrifice was complete, Jesus cried out, "It is finished!" then breathed His last (see John 19:30). With that, the construction of the bridge between sinful man and a holy God had been built, paved, and opened for all of us to cross.

You see, the bridge God built between Himself and us was constructed out of two simple pieces of wood bound together in the form of a cross, and it was paved with the most costly material that ever existed, the precious blood of Jesus Christ.

This is the one and only bridge that gets us to the God we've all been searching for.

THE FINALITY OF BRIDGES

There was a more or less final chapter to the original Lake Washington Floating Bridge. Over the period of half a century after its construction, the bridge gradually but surely wore down. In 1990, as part of a roadway project in the Seattle area, plans were made for a $30 million renovation. But on November 25 of that year, in the midst of the renovation, a heavy rainstorm pounded the Seattle area. Some of those floating concrete pontoons took on water, and about half of this wondrous example of man's ingenuity sank to the bottom of the lake.

In a matter of a few hours, what had been a renovation project became a major restoration and rebuilding project.

That's how it is with man-made bridges, isn't it? No matter how innovatively they are built, no matter how much money we spend, no matter how many skillful people design and build them—eventually they wear out and need to be replaced.

Not so with the bridge God built between His heart and ours. His bridge not only spans the immeasurable gulf between Him and us, but it lasts for all eternity. Because of His wonderful love and compassion for those who know of their need for Him, He has built a bridge to Himself that will never wear out, never collapse, and never need renovation.

It is the only perfect bridge ever built.

And it's the bridge to the God you've been searching for!

REFLECTIONS FOR
INDIVIDUAL OR SMALL GROUP STUDY

1. Spend some time looking through Genesis chapters 1–3. In what ways do you see God revealing Himself? What words would you use to describe God based on this portion of Scripture?

2. How does Genesis 3 set up the whole biblical story straight through the New Testament?

3. What does the author mean by the "otherness" of God?

4. How has culture attempted or succeeded in making God "user-friendly"?

5. Why and how does sin separate us from God?

6. According to this chapter, what is God's solution to this separation?

CHAPTER FOUR

GOD'S LOVE: THE LOVE WE'RE SEARCHING FOR

"There is no one so far lost that Jesus cannot find him and save him."

■ ANDREW MURRAY

THE ELDERLY GENTLEMAN had some serious misgivings about God and what God could possibly want to do with him. To put it bluntly, he just couldn't believe that God loved him.

The man wasn't the worst person you could ever meet; in fact, he was rather likable. But to hear him tell his story, it was obvious he'd done a lot of things he wasn't proud of. He had devoted his life to the pursuit of pleasure and wealth, with little thought of God. Now, in the autumn of his life, he classified himself as one headed anywhere but heaven when he died.

"How could God possibly love me?" he asked. "I've wasted most of my life. How could He love me, accept me, and forgive someone like me? Wouldn't He be better off spending His time on better people?"

When I hear these kinds of questions, it reminds me that most of us aren't just searching for *a* god, but for *the* God who truly loves and accepts and cares for us on a personal level. Problem is, many of us—even Bible-believing Christians—wonder how a holy God can love us, with all our flaws and imperfections.

I wonder about that myself sometimes. That's right! A man who has devoted his life to full-time service for God has moments when he questions God's love, when he wonders if the Lord really cares for him as deeply as He says. When those doubts and questions creep in, God gives me all the assurance I need of His love for me. Through His Word and through His acts toward me, He sends me the message, "I love *you*, Mac Brunson!"

If you want to see a picture of the character and personality of God, if you want to see how He really feels about you, then you need only look where I look for assurance of His love: to His written Word, the Bible. That's where you read of His wisdom, of His power, and of His works. And it's where you read of His wonderful love.

THE LOOK OF GOD'S LOVE

I've spent a large portion of my life studying the Bible, and I've discovered many wondrous things about the attributes and character of God. For example, when I read of His wisdom, I discover some things about His mind—particularly that it is infinitely above even the most brilliant human intellect.

When I read of God's works, I see His awesome power, which is far and above anything we can describe or even imagine.

But when I read in the Bible of God's incredible love, I see what is most important to all of us who are searching for a God who loves us—His heart.

The Bible tells us over and over that God's heart, His very inner being, is one of love. Yes, God is the only One who is completely holy and righteous, the only One who has absolute power and rule, the only One who could create all we see around us with but a word. But He is also the only One who is perfect and complete love. As the apostle so simply put it, "God *is* love" (1 John 4:8, emphasis added).

As difficult as it is at times for my human mind to comprehend, this all-knowing, all-powerful God— the God who knows all and who put everything from the cosmos to the most delicate flower in place— loves *us*. It's right there in the Book.

HOW GOD LOVES YOU!

At first, you might find some of the things about God's love a bit hard to believe. Maybe you've never really considered the kind of love I'm talking about, or maybe you've never enjoyed in an earthly relationship the kind of acceptance and love He has for you. But read on—and you will be blessed to your very soul as you see what the Word says about the depth and breadth of His love for you.

Here are some of the specific things the Bible says about God's love for you.

God Loves You Personally

When you think of the words "God's love," which Bible verse comes to mind? For many people, it's likely John 3:16, which tells us that, "For God so loved the world, that He gave His only begotten Son. . . ." This verse has become a big part of our culture. Even those with little knowledge of the Bible seem to know it. It is a beautiful word picture of God's love and what He did to express that love.

But this verse, as beautiful as it is, doesn't directly address what I consider a vital aspect of God's love. You see, God doesn't just love the world *collectively*; He loves you and me *individually*.

By faith, by believing in my heart and mind what God's Word tells me, I know that God loves me personally. When I read John 3:16, I feel completely comfortable with personalizing it: "For God so loved *Mac Brunson*, that He gave His only begotten Son. . . ."

The apostle Paul understood God's personal love as well as anyone. He was a man who had, prior to his meeting Christ on the road to Damascus, made a life of trying to stamp out this "new" religion called Christianity. But he knew that the love God poured out on the world He also poured out on Paul individually and personally: "*I* have been crucified with Christ; and it is no longer *I* who live, but Christ lives in *me*; and the life which *I* now live in the flesh *I* live by faith in the Son of God, who loved *me* and delivered Himself up for *me*" (Galatians 2:20, emphasis added).

That verse makes this whole love-of-God thing very personal, doesn't it? And it underscores what Christianity is all about—a personal love relationship with almighty God Himself.

And there's nothing we can do to make that love go away.

God Loves You Unconditionally

Several years ago I gave my wife, Deb, a black-and-tan cocker spaniel, and two years later she gave me a platinum cocker. This breed of dog is *very* loyal. No matter where we go or what we're doing, they are constantly under our feet. And no matter what kind of day I've had or how tired, grouchy, quiet, or indifferent I seem to be, our dogs are always at my side, wagging their tails and waiting to give and receive some loving.

Sadly, the love of most humans can't compare to the unconditional love of a dog! How you look, how you smell, how you talk, how you think, and how you behave *does* matter to other people. When it comes to human relationships, most are "if-then" arrangements: *If* you do this, *then* I'll love you and value you.

Not so with the love of God. That's because He loves not on the basis of who or what we are but on who He is.

The apostle John wrote, "We love, because He first

loved us" (1 John 4:19). This means that God extended His love to us even though we weren't worthy, even before we considered Him or gave a relationship with Him any thought. There are no boundaries or limits to God's love. He loves us no matter what we do, no matter what we become, and no matter who we are.

God's love is perfect because it is not dependent on human effort or accomplishment. There is nothing we can do to strengthen, deepen, or weaken His love for us. It is always immovably in place, looking for ways to reach out to us.

Now *that's* the perfect picture of unconditional love.

God Knows You Through and Through and Still Loves You

When do we people usually find someone most delightful or lovable? Most of the time, when we first meet that person. Call it a "honeymoon" period in any kind of relationship; it's that time when we find out what we have in common with someone and how enjoyable he or she is to be around.

This often changes, however, when we really get to *know* someone—when we start to see that person's quirks, habits, and imperfections. This is often when we start to wonder if the person we have met is everything we thought he or she was. Sometimes these revelations about the person spell the end of what was in the beginning a promising relationship.

I want to assure you now that you never have to

worry about that happening with God. He knows us, knows *everything* about us—the good, the bad, and the ugly—and He still loves us with an undying love.

You see, God knows we are sinners. Yes, He knows about our talents, skills, and gifts. After all, He's the One who gave us those things. But He also knows about our every sinful action, about our every impure thought, about our wrong motivations, about our selfishness.

God knows all these things, and He *loves us anyway!* He loves us because it is His nature to love the unlovable. He loves us because, as fallen and sinful and depraved as we are, we are His children, and it is His nature to pour out love on those who most need it.

The apostle Paul summarized this love perfectly when he wrote, "God demonstrates His own love toward us, in that *while we were yet sinners,* Christ died for us" (Romans 5:8, emphasis added).

Furthermore, it is God's nature not just to love us, but to actually rejoice over us!

God Delights in You

I'm the father of three wonderful children who truly are the apple of my eye. No matter what my children do—at home, at school, in the work world—I will always feel that way about them. Deb and I have one daughter who is serving in the Middle East as a missionary, and two sons, one in college and one in high school. Both of our boys lead Bible studies at church and at school.

Of course I'm pleased when my children succeed or do good for others, but there is nothing they can do to make themselves more special to me. And there is nothing they can do to make me love them less.

I will always delight in my children, but as much as I rejoice in them, I believe that my rejoicing over them is absolute sulking compared to the way God rejoices over us.

One of the prophets in the Old Testament had some beautiful words to say about how God rejoices over us: "The LORD your God is in your midst, A victorious warrior. He will *exult* over you with joy, He will be quiet in His love, He will *rejoice* over you with shouts of joy" (Zepheniah 3:17, emphasis added).

It's right there in writing! God is shouting and rejoicing and delighting over you at this very moment, *celebrating* over you. It's one thing to love someone, but actually *delighting* in that person is another thing altogether. That means not just loving someone—selflessly caring for their physical, emotional, and spiritual needs—but actually *liking and enjoying* that person . . . *just because you do.*

That's how God feels about you and me.

I know what you're thinking: *Preacher, are you trying to tell me that God—the all-powerful, all-knowing, almighty Creator—actually likes me and enjoys me?* That's *exactly* what I'm saying!

King David, who went through his own struggles with doubts concerning acceptance and confidence before God, said it this way: "He brought me forth also into a broad place; He rescued me, because He delighted in me" (Psalm 18:19).

Can anything give us more confidence concerning God's love than knowing He *delights* in us and wants us to come near Him? We all need to take hold of the fact that God loves us personally and unconditionally, that He knows everything about us yet delights in us.

And we need to take hold of the fact that all perfect love flows *from* Him.

GOD IS A FOUNTAIN OF LOVE

Recently, as I was flying into Houston, Texas, I saw a huge fountain in front of one of the city's sports complexes. It caught my eye not just because of its beauty but because of its size. As the plane made its way over the fountain and toward the airport, it occurred to me that this huge fountain was *self-feeding,* meaning that water flows both *from* it and *into* it. In other words, no one needed to add water to this fountain—it supplied its own.

As I thought about that fountain later, I realized that it was a great illustration of one of the attributes of God's love. Love—an infinite supply of love, because God Himself is infinite—flows freely from Him to us, through us to others, then back to Him.

It has been said that "Love isn't love until you give it away." That is exactly how God has designed His love to work. John tells us that God's purpose in giving us love is for us to pass it on to others: "Beloved, let us love one another, for love is from God" (1 John 4:7).

God has given me incredible love for the people around me. Not only do I love my wife and children with all my heart, but I love the people God has placed in my life as friends, relatives, and congregation. I can honestly say that I serve as a pastor not for the paycheck or because I enjoy preaching—although both are nice benefits—but because I genuinely love the people I serve.

I know I have this kind of love only because my heavenly Father, the fountain of all perfect love, showers me with it. And since He's done that, I can't help but pass it on to others.

That's not to say that this world doesn't have its own kinds of love. We humans, as fallen and selfish as we are, have the capacity to demonstrate certain kinds of love.

HUMAN LOVE—NOT ALL BAD, BUT NOT PERFECT, EITHER!

Jesus spoke of one kind of human love when He said, "If you were of the world, the world would love its own" (John 15:19). In the original language, this love is called *phileo*, and it's an affectionate, "brotherly" love—the kind of love you would have for a good friend. It's the love that motivates people, whether they're believers or not, to perform acts of charity and kindness for other people.

The other human love is the kind most of the world is familiar with: romantic or erotic love—the kind between a man and a woman. That's the love we see depicted in the movies and on television, as well as in the Old Testament book Song of Solomon. It's a love based on physical, mental, and emotional attraction. It's a love we can fall into and, sadly, a love we can fall out of.

I don't want to suggest that there is anything necessarily wrong with these kinds of love. Both can add a great deal of joy and happiness to our lives. I know they have to mine. I feel a great deal of brotherly love for some very close friends; and of course, I've enjoyed a years-long romantic love with my wife. These relationships are blessings from God. I love my friends, and I can't imagine being married to anyone but the woman the Lord has brought into my life.

But even at their very best, these kinds of love are incomplete and imperfect simply because they spring from my fallen human heart. I know that apart from the love of God, my love for others could very well be fickle, flighty, and oftentimes based on what the other person could do for me.

God's love is different from my love—vastly different!

GOD'S LOVE—UNLIKE ANY OTHER!

The word for the love of God as it appears in 1 John 4:7 is *agape*. It is the love unique to Christianity, because it's the love that comes directly from God. It's a completely giving, self-sacrificing love. It is not fickle or impulsive, and it doesn't spring out of the merits of the individual receiving the love but from the heart of the one giving the love (see 1 Corinthians 13).

This is God's love, the love that moved Him to look at you and me and say to us, "I love you, and I'm going to give everything I have to bring you back to me. It's going to hurt more than you can imagine, because I'm going to send my Son to die for you. But I'm doing that because I care more about you than I do about my own feelings."

The apostle James points out that this is a love we can absolutely count on: "Every good thing given and every perfect gift is from above, coming down from the Father of lights, with whom there is no variation or shifting shadow" (James 1:17). That tells us that God never changes and that there is no fickleness or "up and down" to His love. He will never abandon us or turn His back on us when we need Him.

It's an amazing, almost incomprehensible love, and it's even more so to us when we take a close look at what the Bible says about it. All of that love flows from God in high heaven—in His words and, more importantly, in His deeds.

GOD'S LOVE IS LOVE IN ACTION

We all want to be loved, but more than mere *words* of love—as important as those are—we want *demonstrations* of love. We want a love we can see and not just hear about, a love backed up by action.

That's the kind of love God has showered on us. He did not just tell us He loved us; He showed us. John wrote of the action behind His words of love: "By this the love of God was manifested in us, that God has sent His only begotten Son into the world so that we might live through Him. In this is love, not that we loved God, but that He loved us and sent His Son to be the propitiation for our sins" (1 John 4:9–10).

The word *propitiation* means the payment of a debt. In this passage, the payment is for the debt of our sin, and it is inseparably linked to the work of Jesus Christ on the cross—the ultimate act of selflessness and love.

God didn't try to win our hearts with just words. He didn't just send us a card, a box of candy, and flowers to let us know He was thinking of us. Yes, He sent His own love letter, the Bible, to *tell* us how much He loves us and delights in us. But He also gave us a tangible, visible picture of His love when He put His Son on a cross for the whole world to see.

But that wasn't the end of it, for God the Father continues to lovingly care for His children, even when we sin against Him.

GOD'S LOVE IS A RESCUING LOVE

I'm so glad that God continues to love me and care for me—even when I stumble and fall. I have no doubt that it is during those times that God pours out an extra portion of His love.

God gave me an unforgettable illustration of this one Sunday morning years ago as I prepared to preach. It was at the time of my first church assignment after seminary, and I scurried around the house getting myself ready. It was almost time for us to leave, but as I walked into the bedroom, I saw something I thought would rock my whole world.

Our daughter, Courtney—just a little crawler at the time—had gotten into my wife's makeup basket and had eaten a whole bottle of mascara. When I walked into the room, Courtney, holding the near-empty mascara bottle in her little hand, smiled up at me with lips and teeth covered in black. She had the stuff running down the side of her face from her mouth, which looked like an empty black hole.

Looking back on it now, it was a funny scene. Not so at the time! Being a young father, I was sure she had poisoned herself. In a near panic, I grabbed her up and bolted out of the room, hollering for Debbie. At that point, my concern for my daughter's health and life pushed out of my mind any thoughts of preaching that morning.

Debbie took our daughter from me as I frantically called the pediatrician to find out what I needed to do. When I got the doctor on the phone, I took the mascara bottle in my hand and read off the ingredients.

"Mr. Brunson, just calm down," he said in a soothing tone. "It won't hurt her. Just clean out her mouth and wash her face. She'll be fine."

With great relief flooding my heart and mind, I took Courtney to the kitchen sink and began cleaning her up. She squirmed and struggled and fussed at me as I took a warm, wet washcloth and cleaned her mouth and face. With that finished, I put her down—

then kept an eye on her so she couldn't get into any more of my wife's makeup!

Let me ask you a question about my response to my daughter's situation. Do you think that when I looked at her with that gunk in her mouth that I loved her one bit less? Was there even a small part of me that wanted to say, "I've got to get to church, so you're on your own"? Absolutely not! In fact, at the very moment—when I believed Courtney's health or even life could be in danger—I was more interested and concerned about her than ever. She had my undivided attention.

If you are a parent, this may not sound like a very noteworthy story. No doubt, you've had to clean up your share of messes. But to me, this story is about more than giving a child the attention needed when he or she makes a mess of things. It's also an illustration of God's love and how we often perceive it.

When we "make a mess of things"—that is, when we sin—our God doesn't lose interest in us. He doesn't sit on His throne and say, "Tsk, tsk! You've done it again! When will you ever learn? Well, you got yourself into this mess, so you can get yourself out of it! I have more important things to do than clean up after you."

Sadly, that's how many Christians perceive the love of God. When we sin, the condemnation comes, and we begin to think that there's no way God can still love us as much as He did before. So instead of running to the Father for cleansing and forgiveness like we need to, we run away and hide from Him.

I firmly believe that the times when sin has its hold on us are the times when God is most keenly interested in us. Just as my daughter had my undivided attention after eating that bottle of mascara, we have God's undivided attention when we fall, when we feel defeated, when we think there is no way a holy God could ever want anything to do with us.

And just as I took the time to clean up my daughter after she made a mess of herself, God takes the time to clean us up—from the inside out—when we sin. But more than that, when He finishes cleaning us up, He reaches down and fills us with His Spirit so that we can be empowered to be the kind of people He wants us to be and live the way He wants us to live.

That, friends, is a picture of perfect love . . . of God's love.

REFLECTIONS FOR
INDIVIDUAL OR SMALL GROUP STUDY

1. What is unconditional love?

2. Why is the idea of a loving God so difficult for people to embrace?

3. In what ways does the Bible say that God "delights" in His children?

4. How does God show His unconditional love to humanity?

5. If we are related to such an all-loving God, how should this relationship impact our earthly relationships?

6. How does Jesus demonstrate the love-qualities of God?

CHAPTER FIVE

THE MIGHTY, GENTLE HAND OF GOD

Have Thine own way, Lord!
Have Thine own way!
Thou art the Potter, I am the clay.

■ GEORGE C. STEBBINS

IF WE HAVEN'T SAID IT to someone else, we've had it said to us in a moment of trouble or crisis: "Just leave it in the hands of the Lord."

Sometimes that little bit of advice comes when we have nothing else helpful to say. But at the same time, it is a great statement of faith. That's because only God's hands are big enough to hold the whole world and at the same time handle our problems and trials. The world cannot throw anything at us—no trial too big, no problem so serious—that we can't put it in God's hands, knowing that He has as His heart's desire what is best for us.

We can be assured that when God extends His hand to us, we can reach back and take it, knowing that His hand is more than capable of tending to our every need.

After all, His are the hands that hold all we see around us.

HANDS OF MAJESTY AND POWER

When it comes to handshakes, which kind makes you most comfortable: the weak "cold fish" handshake or a firm-yet-gentle grip? Obviously, the firm-but-gentle handshake tells you that the one offering the hand has strength and power but also a gentle, compassionate side.

That sounds like the hand of God we're talking about, doesn't it?

The prophet Isaiah had some incredible things to say about the hand of God: "Who has measured the waters in the hollow of His hand, And marked off the heavens by the span . . . ?" (Isaiah 40:12).

To give you an idea of the power and majesty Isaiah is talking about here, I want to point out that the world's five oceans and more than sixty seas cover about 70 percent of the Earth's surface. The Pacific Ocean alone covers more than 155 million square miles with an average depth of more than 13,000 feet. Its deepest point, in what is called the Mariana Trench, located east of the Mariana Islands, is more than 36,000 feet—almost seven miles—deep.

If that weren't enough to ponder, try to imagine the vastness of the universe. Compared with the rest of the cosmos, the planet we live on, with a diameter of just over 7,900 miles at the equator, is but a tiny speck of dust. The Milky Way galaxy, of which our solar system is a part, contains some two hundred billion stars and countless other celestial objects. Astronomers tell us that the Milky Way measures about 100,000 light years across, meaning it would take a beam of light, traveling at 186,000 miles *per second,* 100,000 years to travel from one outer edge of the galaxy to the other. And if that doesn't boggle your mind, consider this: our galaxy is one of literally *billions* of galaxies in the universe.

All of this helps us realize how small we really are . . . and how big our God is.

When you consider that the God who loves you and cares for you in every way is the same God the Bible says holds this awesome, magnificent universe in the hollow of His very hand, you can't help but know that there is nothing in your life He can't handle.

GOD'S SHAPING HAND

If there is one part of God's character most people don't like thinking about, it is His hand of discipline.

When you put the words *discipline* and *God* in the same sentence, it can sound pretty ominous, can't it? Yet the Bible contains many references to this kind of discipline. For example: "If you will not listen to the voice of the LORD, but rebel against the command of the LORD, then the hand of the LORD will be against you" (1 Samuel 12:15). This warning of judgment, as frightening as it may be, is only a small part of the story of God's discipline that we all need to see and understand.

Wrong Ideas about Discipline

Many people, including a lot of Christians, have the wrong idea about how and why God disciplines His people. We may acknowledge that God loves us and that He sent His Son to die for us, and we may have a general idea about the Holy Spirit and His role in our Christian walk. But somehow, in the back of our minds, we have this picture of God as some big celestial ogre, ready to pounce on us the minute we step out of line.

In the MGM classic *The Wizard of Oz*, Dorothy, the Lion, the Scarecrow, and the Tin Man approach the Wizard hoping to receive something important to them. But as they approach, they are greeted by an explosion of fire and huge billowing puffs of green smoke. When the smoke finally clears, a great menacing majestic head shouts at them and orders them to step forth. Each one steps forward to tell the Wizard what he or she needs but is interrupted by this omniscient ogre. He shouts to the Scarecrow, "You have the effrontery to ask for a brain, you billowing bale of bovine fodder!"

Sadly, many of us have a *Wizard of Oz* impression of God. We believe that He is all fire and smoke and dread, with no love or mercy and no understanding of human weakness. Like the Wizard of Oz, who was only a huge head with no real power to grant the wishes of those who approached him, we think God is just a God of punishment and discipline with no hand of compassion.

But that is as far from the truth as you can get about God's hand of discipline.

No one enjoys being disciplined, particularly by the hand of God. But if we fully understand that this discipline comes from the hand of a loving heavenly Father who wants the very best for us, while we may not enjoy the discipline, we'd welcome it!

As most moms and dads know, parental discipline isn't fun, and sometimes it's not pretty. There were times when it shattered my heart to have to mete out different kinds of discipline for my children. But at the same time, there was no way that I—a father who loves his children more than I can put into words—could neglect that part of my responsibility as a parent. I love my kids too much to do that.

The same is true of the God we serve.

The author of the epistle to the Hebrews spoke very directly to this when he wrote, "'My son, do not regard lightly the discipline of the Lord, Nor faint when you are reproved by Him; For those whom the Lord loves He disciplines, And He scourges every son whom He receives.' . . . God deals with you as with sons; for what son is there whom his father does not discipline?" (Hebrews 12:5–7).

This passage goes on to tell us that if we aren't enduring some discipline from God, then it may very well be because we aren't one of His children in the first place (v. 8).

The most wonderful thing about God's discipline is that He, unlike earthly parents, knows perfectly not just what we need as far as discipline is concerned, but how much we can take. It's a perfect discipline in that it springs out of His perfect love.

This is a shaping, molding kind of discipline. And it has always been a part of God's character, as we can see in the Old Testament book of Isaiah.

Discipline: Old Testament Style

Isaiah 1–39 deals with some not-too-pleasant pictures of coming discipline. While Isaiah does promise better times and blessings in the future, this section of the Old Testament offers repeated predictions of judgment from God on His people. The Lord tells the people that because of their rebellion and idolatry, they will be taken into captivity.

Isaiah's warning concerning God's discipline—sometimes *severe* discipline—wasn't the first the people of Israel had heard. Clear back in the book of Deuteronomy, we read of Moses receiving God's warnings at Mount Gerizim. Moses read the blessings that would come on the people and the nation as long as they worshiped the Lord, but he also read the curses that would befall them if they were disobedient: "The LORD will bring a nation against you from afar, from the end of the earth, as the eagle swoops down, a nation whose language you shall not understand" (Deuteronomy 28:49).

That's part of how God's hand of discipline works. Patience and repeated warnings, followed by judgment. That kind of discipline, the Bible tells us, is in keeping with His character: "'The LORD, the LORD God, compassionate and gracious, slow to anger, and abounding in lovingkindness and truth; who keeps lovingkindness for thousands, who forgives iniquity, transgression and sin; yet He will by no means leave the guilty unpunished'" (Exodus 34:6–7).

THE LOOK OF THE LORD'S DISCIPLINE

Through the story of King David's sin and restoration, God gives us a beautiful picture of His hand of discipline and why He lays that hand—sometimes very heavily—on those He loves.

David found out that it's not a pleasant experience to be under the disciplining hand of the Lord. David had sinned against God, big-time. He had committed adultery, and then he tried to cover his tracks by having the woman's husband killed in battle. He didn't get away with it, though. He wrote, "When I kept silent about my sin, my body wasted away Through my groaning all day long. For day and night Your hand was heavy upon me" (Psalm 32:3–4). Some of David's psalms from this time in his life expressed such misery that he actually accused God of abandoning him!

In short order, David had broken two of God's commandments, and it was time for God to lay His hand of discipline on him. It came in the form of the prophet Nathan, who lovingly but firmly confronted the king about his sin (2 Samuel 12).

David did the only thing he could do: Confess. He prayed, "I acknowledged my sin to You, And my iniquity I did not hide; I said, 'I will confess my transgressions to the LORD'; And You forgave the guilt of my sin" (Psalm 32:5). David still faced the consequences of his sin, but his relationship with God was restored.

This story teaches us two things. First, God will not allow His people to get away with sin. He loves us too much to allow that to happen. We may try to hide our wrongdoing from public view, but God knows our hearts and all our actions. And when we step out of line, He will always discipline us in some fashion.

Second, God disciplines those He loves—just as He disciplined King David, the "man after God's own heart" (1 Samuel 13:13–14). As miserable as David became over his sin and as severe as the consequences were, the discipline from above was for his own good and for the good of God's kingdom.

We need to see God's discipline not as a curse and not as Him coming down on us but as His way of keeping us in line with His will or correcting some sinful way or attitude or heart condition. And we need to see this discipline as an act of love and not condemnation.

Do you look at the trials and tests in your life and wonder if God is sending discipline your way? That may very well be, so you should rejoice, not complain or grumble. For it is further evidence that God sees you as worth the time and effort to make changes and corrections. As the writer of Hebrews pointed out, it is proof that He loves you and is concerned about you.

No one, including God Himself, expects you to *enjoy* His hand of discipline. On the contrary, the apostle wrote, "All discipline for the moment seems not to be joyful, but sorrowful; yet to those who have been trained by it, afterwards it yields the peaceful fruit of righteousness" (Hebrews 12:11).

If you believe you are under God's hand of discipline, I want you to understand that there are four specific things He is trying to accomplish on your behalf.

Correct and Train Us

In our culture, we tend to use the word *discipline* interchangeably with the word *punishment*. Sometimes discipline carries with it an element of punishment—as you have already read—but it also means to correct, reprove, train, and instruct.

The apostle Paul tells us that God disciplines us so that we can remain set apart from the world around us: "We are disciplined by the Lord so that we will not be condemned along with the world" (1 Corinthians 11:32).

You may have heard someone who is under God's discipline lament, "Sometimes I think God hates me!" But that is as far from the truth as can be. No man or woman is more blessed than the one God lovingly takes the time to correct and train. And when we realize that God is doing that for us, we can rest even more assured that He values us and loves us.

Convict Us of Sin

It's easy to look around the world and see all the sinning that goes on and feel grieved and maybe a little outraged. But the world's sinfulness shouldn't shock us or surprise us. After all, sinners do one thing better than anything else: sin! And we do it boldly and openly!

Jesus told His disciples that one of the missions of the Holy Spirit was to convict the world of sin (John 16:8). The Holy Spirit's role in the life of the believer is to act as the disciplining hand of God by letting us know when we are on the right track, or when we step out of line. As Jesus said, "He will guide you into all the truth" (v. 13).

God has promised us that He will let us know when we step off course and away from Him. David wrote, "Search me, O God, and know my heart; Try me and know my anxious thoughts; And see if there be any hurtful way in me, And lead me in the everlasting way" (Psalm 139:23–24). We can rest assured that the Lord, through His Holy Spirit, will do just that for us.

Mold and Shape Us

Have you ever seen what can happen to a formless, shapeless lump of clay in the hands of a fine potter? This skilled artisan takes what was once unattractive and useless and turns it into a beautiful, useful piece of pottery.

The potter starts by spinning the clay on a potter's wheel. Using a delicate, knowing touch that comes from years of experience, she can shape that piece of clay into the near-perfect form of a vase or pot. But it doesn't end there. Once the clay has been formed and has air-dried, the potter uses her "tools of the trade" to knock off and sand off all the flaws and imperfections. Finally, once she has perfected the piece, it is ready for the kiln. What was once nothing more than a hunk of dirt becomes a fine work of art.

Isaiah uses this picture metaphorically when he writes of God's disciplining hand in our lives: "We are the clay, and You our potter; And all of us are the work of Your hand" (Isaiah 64:8). When we begin to see ourselves as clay in our Master's hand, we will also begin to see His discipline as a blessing, something we should actually *seek* and not avoid.

Transform and Remake Us

Years ago, a popular bumper sticker said, "Please Be Patient. God Isn't Finished with Me Yet." Indeed He is not! The apostle Paul tells us that this transformation is an ongoing process that God is carrying out on those He loves: "But we all . . . are being transformed into the same image from glory to glory, just as from the Lord, the Spirit" (2 Corinthians 3:18).

Jeremiah wrote of this transformation, again using the potter metaphor: "But the vessel that He was making of clay was spoiled . . . so He *remade* it into another vessel, as it pleased the potter to make" (Jeremiah 18:4, emphasis added).

In nature, we see many wonderful examples of remaking, or transformation. The caterpillar transforms itself into a beautiful butterfly, the tadpole into a frog, and the stone fly nymph into an adult stone fly.

All of these are wonderful miracles of a God-created nature. But none approaches the beauty of the transformation God does in us. At the moment we put our faith in Jesus Christ for salvation, we are transformed. We are no longer what we were before. But there's more. God uses His Spirit, His written Word, and His acts of discipline to transform and retransform us until we become what He wants us to be: earthly pictures of Himself.

That, friends, is the reason God disciplines us.

And that discipline, as difficult as it may be to endure at times, is always followed by His acts of comfort.

GOD'S HAND OF COMFORT

Most parents know it's not pleasant to have to discipline their children. I never enjoyed disciplining my kids, but I knew that discipline was necessary if my children were to grow up to be the people they are today.

I also knew that after I had disciplined my children, there had to be that time of reconciliation, that time of comfort for them, so that they would know that even though I was not pleased with something they had done, I had forgiven them and loved them as much as ever, if not more.

I believe we can rest assured that when God puts His hand of discipline on us—when He punishes or corrects us—He will later follow that by stretching out His hand to comfort us.

Isaiah addresses the comforting hand of God: "Speak kindly to Jerusalem; And call out to her, that her warfare has ended, That her iniquity has been removed, That she has received of the LORD's hand Double for all her sins" (Isaiah 40:2).

In the King James Version, this same verse starts out "Comfort ye, comfort ye my people." This is representative of God the Father reaching down to comfort a people—a people enduring great distress and trouble—whom He has had to discipline, *at the very time they were enduring the punishment!*

This says some wonderful things about the God who reaches out His hand of discipline. It tells us that God has great compassion on His people, even when they rebel against Him. It tells us that it was important to Him that they be comforted. And it tells us that even in the midst of God's most severe discipline, He will never disown or turn His back on those He loves. Even after He has given them over to slavery and distress, He still calls these rebels "My people."

This is a beautiful picture of God intervening on behalf of His people and making a way for them to be reconciled to Him . . . and a way for Him to bless them.

GOD'S HAND OF
INTERVENTION AND BLESSING

We've all heard of interventions. That is when a group of people get together with a friend or family member to confront that person about something destructive in his or her life—say a drug or alcohol problem. Their hope is to help that person remove the addiction from his or her life.

Likewise, God intervenes on behalf of those He has disciplined. But instead of *helping* His people rid themselves of their sin, He does it Himself. And not only that, He actually takes the time to bless those He has had to discipline.

The Lord's words in Isaiah 40:2, "That her iniquity has been removed, That she has received of the LORD's hand Double for all her sins," speak of that kind of intervention. In this context the word *removed* means literally that His people's iniquity has been paid for, that their sin has been wiped away.

At first glance, it sounds as though God's people are being punished twice for their sins. But that is not the case. You see, in this passage, the word *double* refers to the idea of a double blessing—simply because God intervened, wiped away the people's sins, and restored them.

Then comes the blessing!

We can see this demonstrated in the life of King David. At one time, he followed God closely and did great things for Him. Then he fell into sin. But God never abandoned David or gave up on him. Rather, He put His hand of discipline on the king, forgave him and restored him, then blessed him greatly (see Psalm 18:16–17, 35–36).

The intervention spoken of in Isaiah 40 is a prelude to this great Messianic passage: "Surely our griefs He Himself bore, And our sorrows He carried" (Isaiah

53:4). This passage speaks of the coming Messiah, the One God would sacrifice on a cross so that we could have the hand of God on our lives for the rest of our earthly existence and into eternity.

God has stretched out His hand to us by offering up His Son for us. When we stretch out our own hands to take His, we get to enjoy this wonderful promise: "Behold, I have inscribed you on the palms of My hands" (Isaiah 49:16).

We can rest in God's hands, knowing that He is mighty enough and big enough to save us, forgive us, care for us, and look out for us and warn us when we are about to fall. And if we *do* fall, we know He'll pick us up, cleanse us, then bless us as never before.

Resting in the hand of God. That is the ultimate place of fulfillment and blessing.

REFLECTIONS FOR
INDIVIDUAL OR SMALL GROUP STUDY

1. What in this chapter surprised you about God?

2. How do you feel about God disciplining His children?

3. How would you explain to someone the biblical differences between divine punishment and divine discipline? Give some examples of both.

4. How does our society's view of discipline and justice undermine or support our understanding of God's loving discipline?

5. Should churches discipline believers for sinful behavior? Why or why not?

6. How does God deal with unbelievers who do evil or shameful things?

CHAPTER SIX

THE GOD
WHO FORGIVES

*Faith alone justifies and fulfills the
law; and this because faith brings us
the spirit gained by the merits of
Christ.*

■ MARTIN LUTHER

LON WAS A GOOD JEWISH BOY from a good Jewish
family. He went to synagogue every Sabbath, read the
Torah fluently in Hebrew, and was bar mitzvahed at age
thirteen. He believed deeply in God and that one day he
would be accepted into heaven because he was a son of
Abraham.

At age fifteen, however, Lon lost interest in his faith.
He began to see religion as irrelevant to his life. So
instead of going to the synagogue with his Jewish brothers and sisters, he started hanging out with the wrong
kind of people, who introduced him to partying and
alcohol.

After high school, Lon enrolled in the University of
North Carolina as a chemistry major. He joined a fraternity that was 50 percent Jewish, but almost 100 percent

partiers. He plunged deeply into the party scene, and soon what had been to him social drinking became an addiction. Lon was an alcoholic.

But things got worse.

In 1969, Lon headed off for Woodstock, where he had his first experiences with LSD. He was convinced that he had found meaning in life through the hallucinogenic drug—so convinced that when he returned to campus he influenced a majority of his fraternity brothers to try it. In time, he became one of the leading drug pushers at Chapel Hill.

As he sank deeper into the drug culture at the university, Lon became more detached from his original purpose in going there. He began to miss classes and fail quizzes. Nothing his professors said to him seemed to have any effect. He became the first student ever to flunk out of the UNC honors program in chemistry.

Lon's life was falling apart, and he knew it. He felt directionless and worthless. His only comfort came from the drugs, which only temporarily numbed the pain of his existence. One day, he told a friend that instead of getting better as a person, as he thought he would when he started using LSD, he was getting worse. What that friend told Lon shook his world.

"Lon, maybe you are not getting worse," the friend said. "Maybe you are just getting honest with who you have been all along."

Lon wanted change. He realized that he wasn't going to find the real meaning to life in drugs, so he began looking for it in religion—Taoism, Confucianism, Buddhism, and others. But none of them removed what he saw as the ugliness in his life. Then he did what many desperate people do: he turned back to what he knew, orthodox Judaism. But he found that the practices of that faith did little to relieve his guilt.

Lon had hit rock bottom, and religion wasn't helping. He saw himself as a bad person, a lowlife, and there seemed nothing he could do to change his self-image. He was so miserable, so despondent, that he considered ending his life. But being the procrastinator he was, he put off killing himself.

Then one spring day in 1971, as he walked down one of the campus streets, he saw a van covered with Bible verses. Standing next to the van was a man preaching the Gospel of Christ through a loudspeaker. Students walked by and spit on the man, called him names, and sometimes took the tracts he handed out and tore them up and threw them on the ground.

"Freak!" Lon heard some of the students yell at the man, and he thought they might be right. But the man wouldn't quit. He was at the same street corner every Saturday and Sunday preaching his message. Lon, maybe out of nothing more than curiosity, came to listen to him. Then one day his eyes met this man's, and Lon began to wonder if his message wasn't what he was looking for. Finally, Lon got up the nerve to approach the street preacher and asked if they could talk.

The man smiled warmly at Lon, opened up his

Bible, and spent two hours talking with him about the love and forgiveness of Jesus Christ. He assured Lon that no matter what he'd done, no matter how horrible a person he had been, that God loved him and sent His Son so that he could find forgiveness and peace.

Lon didn't make any commitments on the spot, other than to think and read about what the preacher had told him. He took the Bible the man gave him back to his room and began reading Matthew's Gospel, where he came upon Jesus' words: "Come to Me, all who are weary and heavy-laden, and . . . you will find rest for your souls" (Matthew 11:28–29).

Rest for your souls. That's what I want! Lon said to himself. *That's what I've been looking for!*

In that moment, Lon knew he had found the God he'd been searching for. He asked the Lord to forgive him, to remove the incredible weight of guilt that had tortured his soul, and to give him rest. Not long after, the guilt and turmoil were gone. Lon felt a deep peace and joy he had never known before.

Unable to keep what he had found to himself, Lon followed God's call to train for ministry. He is now a preacher of the Gospel at a church of more than five thousand people in McLean, Virginia.

The world is full of Lons, isn't it? People who know they are sinners but who don't know what to do about it. People looking for the God who forgives.

I believe that each of us—no matter how we are living, no matter how horribly we have behaved in this life—wants to know that we are forgiven, that all our wrongdoing has been erased in the sight of God.

We don't want "warm fuzzies," and we don't want
our sins glossed over. We don't want a God who just
tinkers with us and fixes what's wrong. Rather, we
want a God who forgives, reshapes, and makes us different people from what we once were.

Well, I've got great news for you. The God we've
been searching for is the same God who has taken it on
Himself to remove and never again remember our sins.

If you want to know more about this God of forgiveness, then please read on. I want you to know
about the God who forgives, about how He sees your
sin, and what He's done to remove that sin from your
record.

GOD'S POSITION ON SIN

I want to start this section by telling you something that might make you a bit uncomfortable: The
God you've been searching for, the God of the Holy
Bible, doesn't tolerate sin. He will never ignore or
sidestep it, and He'll never allow us to do so, either. He
is dead serious when it comes to sin. He is a holy God,
and He requires that someone pay for our wrongdoing, no matter how insignificant it may seem in
the big picture of our lives.

To us sinners, that can at first seem like some
pretty harsh or even hopeless news. At this point,
some might even ask themselves, *If I'm a sinner and
God can't accept my sin, what hope can I possibly have?*

You need to know that the God of the Bible *will*
deal with your sin and my sin. But the good news is

that how He deals with that sin is up to you and me. We can choose to have Him deal with our sins through eternal judgment, or we can choose His forgiveness, which He has made available to all who desire it.

In his second letter, the apostle Peter wrote that God is "not wishing for any to perish but for all to come to repentance" (2 Peter 3:9). That tells us something wonderful about God's forgiveness, namely, that He *desires* more than anything to forgive our sins and save us for all of eternity.

Our friend Lon realized something that we need to lay hold of: We will never find forgiveness for our sins through religion or doing good. During a telling conversation with a group of religious leaders called Pharisees, Jesus declared that there is only one way to find forgiveness, and it's through Him: "Unless you believe that I am He [the Christ], you shall die in your sins" (John 8:24).

It's a wonderful paradox that the Lord who can't tolerate our sin has made a way for us to be forgiven for all eternity through the work of Jesus Christ. What exactly does this forgiveness look like? It may surprise you to know that God's forgiveness consists of a whole lot more than just relieving us of guilt and letting go of His anger over our sin.

THE LOOK OF GOD'S FORGIVENESS

Many of us, including many Bible-believing Christians, make the mistake of thinking that the New Testament presents a loving and forgiving God while the Old Testament shows Him to be wrathful and vengeful. This is completely untrue!

The God revealed in Genesis through Malachi is the same God written about in Matthew through Revelation. In *both* Testaments, He is a God of love and forgiveness. In one key Old Testament verse, God identifies Himself as the One who forgives completely: "I, even I, am the one who wipes out your transgressions for My own sake; And I will not remember your sins" (Isaiah 43:25). This one verse tells us that forgiveness rests in God's initiative alone.

God Forgives Sovereignly

In our American culture, we tend to believe that everything should be done democratically. We should get to vote on who represents us, on how our tax money is spent, on whether our nation goes to war. And if we don't get to vote on these things directly, we have a Congress that votes on our behalf, and that vote should reflect "the will of the people."

God's forgiveness isn't done this way. Only one vote matters when it comes to God's forgiveness, and it's His. He forgives simply because He *chooses* to—on His own and without any input from us. That is what He meant when He said that He "wipes out your transgressions for My own sake."

God's forgiveness is an act of His supreme authority, of His sovereignty. No one else—not ourselves, not the local priest, not the pope—has any authority whatsoever to forgive sins. Only God!

David wrote, "Against you, you only, have I sinned" (Psalm 51:4 NIV). In the same psalm, however, David also wrote, "Cleanse me . . . and I will be clean; wash me, and I will be whiter than snow" (v. 7 NIV). This passage shows us that when we sin, we sin against God alone and that He alone can cleanse us and forgive us.

God Forgives Unilaterally

Have you heard the term *unilateral contract?* That's an agreement in which only one of the signees is bound by its terms and conditions. The one not bound by the contract may walk away from the agreement for any reason and at any time. It is, in effect, a one-sided agreement.

God's forgiveness is a lot like that. It is completely unilateral, or one-sided, meaning that He has chosen to be bound to forgiveness *if* we just come to Him and ask. This agreement depends on Him to do the work; it's not an arrangement where He and the sinner work together for the common good. Our only choice in this one-sided arrangement is whether to depend on Him for our forgiveness. If we choose not to do that, God and His forgiveness still stay the same.

This agreement was summed up beautifully by the apostle John, who wrote, "If we confess our sins, He is faithful and righteous to forgive us our sins and to cleanse us from all unrighteousness" (1 John 1:9).

God's Forgiveness Is Unmerited

Many people believe that to be forgiven they need to stop sinning, while others think that if they just do enough good things in life, God will overlook their sin. After all, how could God hold anything against someone who has more stuff on the good side of the balance sheet than on the bad side?

God's forgiveness, though, doesn't look anything at all like that.

Nowhere in Scripture do we read of the Lord saying something like, "You know, I like how you've been serving My people. And I'm pretty pleased that you've given up that little sin we've been talking about. I think I'm going to give you an extra helping of forgiveness. After all, you deserve it!"

On the contrary, forgiveness is completely unmerited. We don't deserve it, and we cannot do anything to make ourselves worthy of it. We can't earn His forgiveness by going to church, by giving more to His ministries, by serving on the mission field, or by doing good for our fellow people.

This is why God's forgiveness is an act of *grace.* God does for us what we don't deserve, and He doesn't do to us what we do deserve.

Paul pointed out that our good works have nothing to do with God's willingness to forgive: "For by grace you have been saved through faith; and that not of yourselves, it is the gift of God; not as a result of works, so that no one may boast" (Ephesians 2:8–9). Paul also tells us that if forgiveness depended on our goodness, then it's not based on grace at all: "But if it is by grace, it is no longer on the basis of works, otherwise grace is no longer grace" (Romans 11:6).

That is so hard for many of us to grasp. We look at our lives and some of the horrible things we've done, and we can't believe that God doesn't expect us to do something to make up for our sin. But God's Word tells us over and over that there is nothing we *can* do to merit His forgiveness. That is poured out on us, not because of who we are, but out of who He is.

GOD'S MOTIVATION FOR FORGIVENESS

Right about now, you may be asking yourself some very serious questions about God, His forgiveness, and how it applies to you personally. You may be wondering, *Why would the God who created everything and controls the world care about forgiving me? Doesn't He know that I'm an imperfect human being and that even if He forgives me, I'll sin again? Why would He waste His time that way?*

Honestly, I struggle with this myself. When I look at my life, I see a man who falls into particular sins time after time and then wonders whether God's forgiveness is wearing thin. He must be tired of my weakness and ready to tell me, "That's it, Brunson! I've had enough! You're on your own!"

When I have these doubts, I have learned to go to God's Word and to God Himself in prayer. Here I receive the assurance that He's not finished with me, that He forgives me and still loves me.

Why does God continually stretch out His hand of forgiveness to a fallen, sinful creature such as me? Why does He continue to extend His hand of grace, even *knowing* that I'm going to fall into sin time and time again? Is it because I'm pitiful and helpless when it comes to my battle with sin and the flesh? Because He feels sorry for me? Because He knows that apart from Him I would be defenseless, the devil's personal punching bag?

These things are certainly true about me, but they aren't why God continues to forgive me. Rather, the gracious acts of kindness and patience that God demonstrates spring from His very character. It honors His holy name to have mercy and forgive. That's what He meant when He said He wipes out our sins and transgressions "for My own sake" (Isaiah 43:25).

I don't know how many times the Lord uses these words or words like them in Scripture. Here are just a few of them:

"He guides me in the paths of righteousness
For His name's sake."
(Psalm 23: 3, emphasis added)

"For the *sake of My name* I delay My wrath . . .
For My own sake, for My own sake, I will act;
For how can *My name* be profaned?"
(Isaiah 48:9, 11, emphasis added)

"Our Father who is in heaven,
Hallowed be Your name."
(Matthew 6:9, emphasis added)

These strong words tell us something essential that we need to know about God: His name is important to Him. The Lord requires that His name always be honored and never defamed, that it be lifted up and never hidden. This, He assures us in Isaiah 43:25, is why He chooses to forgive.

A holy God who cannot tolerate sin could never base His forgiveness on anything about us. I know I can't live this life sinlessly. In fact, even if God were to offer me forgiveness in exchange for some consistency, I'd never be forgiven. If He were to speak to me personally and say, "Mac, I know you can't be perfect, but I'll tell you what. If you can keep from sinning eight out of the ten times you are tempted, then I'll call that good enough." You know what? I'd still be lost—even if I *could* be that consistent.

God would never grade us on a curve. He has one perfect standard, and it is Himself. For that reason, He will never look at our intentions or the sincerity of our hearts in trying to do our best when it comes to our sin.

And praise His name that He doesn't!

If God's forgiveness were based on anything but His desire to glorify His own name, then we'd all be in trouble. We would never know forgiveness, never know pardon.

In those times when we doubt God's ability or

willingness to forgive us, we need only see that we serve a God who will never go back on His word and never fail to glorify His own name.

THE COMPLETENESS OF GOD'S FORGIVENESS

Each of us has that favorite garment in our closet. You know, that shirt, sweater, or coat that stands out above the rest? The one you like to wear to your most important events, simply because it looks so good on you?

Think for a minute about your favorite garment, and try to imagine what you would do if you were to get a stain on it—perhaps coffee, grape juice, or some other food item that leaves a really obvious and stubborn stain. You know you wouldn't want to just place some patch over the stain. So you would use everything within your means—stain removers, your washing machine, and, if worse comes to worst, a professional cleaner—to get the stain out.

This illustrates what God meant when He said, "[I] am the one who wipes out your transgressions" (Isaiah 43:25). In this context, the word *wipes* suggests complete eradication of all the stain of sin. This brings to mind a wonderful word picture of forgiveness early in the book of Isaiah: "'Come now, and let us reason together,' Says the LORD, 'Though your sins are as scarlet, They will be as white as snow; Though they are red like crimson, They will be like wool'" (1:18).

These beautiful words are a metaphorical look at

the process of God's cleansing and forgiveness. And they also point to a literal event we will all personally have to face.

FORGIVENESS: THE ERASER
IN THE HAND OF GOD

The 1991 movie *Defending Your Life* tells the story of a successful and popular man named Daniel who is killed in an accident in the BMW he had just purchased. On "the other side," Daniel finds himself in Judgment City, where he views a less-than-flattering account of his life on earth. Then he has to give an account of everything he had done—and everything he had failed to do.

While this movie is far from theologically correct, the story contains a grain of truth. The Bible tells us that a day will come when each of us must stand before God as He opens the books containing accounts of our lives: "And I saw the dead, the great and the small, standing before the throne, and books were opened; and another book was opened, which is the book of life; and the dead were judged from the things which were written in the books, according to their deeds" (Revelation 20:12).

Each of us, whether or not we intend to, is leaving a spiritual autobiography, one the Bible says will be opened and read aloud come the day of judgment. That's not a pleasant thought for most of us—even those who have lived relatively "clean" lives. But for those of us who have found the freedom of forgiveness in Jesus Christ, there is a hope in that passage of wondrous things to come. Right in the middle of that verse are these words: "and another book was opened, which is the book of life." Later on in Revelation 20, it tells us that those whose names were not found in that book were cast away from God for all of eternity. The rest? That's us—the ones who have found the God who forgives.

Paul tells us that through the work of Jesus Christ on the cross, God has "canceled out the certificate of debt consisting of decrees against us, which was hostile to us; and He has taken it out of the way, having nailed it to the cross" (Colossians 2:14).

There will be judgment for all people according to the things they have done while alive on this earth. For those who haven't received the forgiveness of God, there will be wrath in accordance to all the things recorded in those books John wrote of. But for those who know Jesus Christ, those who have received His gift of forgiveness, the things in those books will be erased from the record.

It will be as though they never existed!

Our Enemy loves to challenge God and us on this point. He loves to entice us to sin, and when we fall, he is right there to condemn us and tell us that what we've done has been etched in granite for all of eternity. "You can't really believe God will erase what you've done!" goes the accusation.

But God tells us otherwise, again through the Old Testament prophet: "'I have wiped out your transgressions like a thick cloud, And your sins like a heavy mist. Return to Me, for I have redeemed you'" (Isaiah 44:22).

Many people, including a lot of Bible-believing Christians, live under a cloud of guilt. Maybe it's over something we did in the distant past, or maybe it's something we are caught up in presently. Sin looms larger and larger as time goes on—with no hope of forgiveness.

But God tells us that it needn't be!

With the wave of His nail-scarred hand, the Lord Jesus sweeps away the dark, ominous clouds of sin that hang over us. When we accept Christ's free, unmerited gift of forgiveness, His light comes in like the rising sun, overwhelming the darkness of our sin. And He gives us the promise that He will remember our sins no more (Isaiah 43:25).

That is the forgiveness we all want and need. And it comes freely from the God we've been searching for.

REFLECTIONS FOR
INDIVIDUAL OR SMALL GROUP STUDY

1. What does forgiveness mean to you?

2. Why do people find it so hard to forgive someone who has wronged them?

3. How do urges to seek revenge hinder our ability to forgive?

4. How is the forgiveness God offers through Jesus different from what we can offer each other? How is it the same?

5. In what ways do you wrestle with accepting God's complete forgiveness?

6. How does knowing God forgives help you forgive yourself?

CHAPTER SEVEN

THE GOD WHO LEADS AND GUIDES

Living a life of faith means never knowing where you are being led. But it does mean loving and knowing the One who is leading.

■ OSWALD CHAMBERS

LIKE MOST PEOPLE LIVING and working in the early twenty-first century, I use a computer most every day. Though I know how to use it, I am far from what you would call computer literate. I know just enough to get by—at least for *most* computer functions.

Those of you who are barely computer functional understand how scary it can be to work on important projects on your computer. I have sat in front of my computer screen many times, absolutely terrified to touch my mouse or keyboard for fear that I'd wipe out important files. And there have been times when I feared I'd erased or lost documents as a deadline approached.

When this happens, it's usually because I just don't know my way around the computer. The files are still there, safe and secure, but I just don't know how to find them. The harder I try to find them, the more I receive messages such as "Access Denied" or "Item Not Found."

Working with a computer can be frustrating for a lot of us, but it's not nearly as frustrating as it sometimes is to determine the will of God. At some point in our lives, each of us has felt as though we have received the "Access Denied" message when we went to God looking for direction.

GOD'S WILL—ACCESS DENIED?

I can't begin to count the number of times when frustrated people of all ages, genders, and walks of life have sat in my office and told me, "Pastor, I just don't know what God wants from me. How can I know His will for my life? How can I get His direction?"

I believe we are all searching for a God who leads and guides us, who actually communicates His will for our own individual lives. I also believe that the search for that God is reflected in our culture's preoccupation with the occult. People of all nations and creeds turn to astrology, tarot cards, mediums, and other forms of communication with the spirit world in order to find meaning and direction in life.

These things are at best a quick fix. More importantly, they are always deceptive. What that person is really looking for—what we are *all* looking for—is a God who leads, guides, and directs us from a place of absolute knowledge, wisdom, and love.

Many of us know from personal experience how

frustrating and, at times, disheartening it can be to feel as though God isn't giving us direction—or if He is, He's not communicating it in a way we can clearly understand. At other times, we believe we have a lead on what God wants from us, but when we move forward, circumstances make us wonder whether it really was God giving us direction.

These kinds of situations are hardly unique to our time. In fact, some of the greatest biblical heroes of the faith struggled with the very same dilemma we do.

Genesis tells us about a young man named Joseph. God had given him great favor with his father plus the ability to receive God's messages in dreams and interpret the dreams of others. Because of all that, Joseph's brothers hated him and, in a fit of jealousy, plotted to kill him. They threw him into a pit, but when a caravan of traders happened by, one of them realized it would be better for them to sell their brother into slavery rather than murder him and get nothing out of it but the satisfaction of being rid of him.

Joseph became the slave of an Egyptian official named Potiphar. He didn't do badly at Potiphar's house at all! In fact, God gave him favor in his master's eyes, and he enjoyed great success. But that changed when Potiphar's wife tried to seduce him. When Joseph refused her advances and fled from her—leaving behind his clothing which she ripped off him—she accused him of trying to force himself on her, and Potiphar had him imprisoned. Joseph served his master faithfully, and he wound up in a jail cell (see Genesis 37, 39)!

I wonder what went through the mind of Moses as

he and many thousands of his people stood at the shore of the Red Sea with Pharaoh's army bearing down on them. God had given Moses clear direction and then miraculously delivered the children of Israel out of slavery in Egypt. But now, the sounds of hoof-beats and chariot wheels grew louder and louder. A terrified crowd begged Moses to lead them back to the safety—as well as the bondage—of Egypt. With the depths of the sea standing between him and the realization of God's appointed task, Moses wanted to stay right where he was. But neither of these options was within the will of God. Moses and his people were about to find out that the Lord wasn't finished showing them, as well as the Egyptians, His power (see Exodus 14).

We also see an example of this in the New Testament. Acts 16 records that the apostle Paul attempted to travel to Asia and then to Bithynia to preach, but the Holy Spirit thwarted his plans (Acts 16:6–7). So instead, Paul traveled to the seaport city of Troas, where he received a vision from God concerning his future.

I can't help but think that there were moments during these episodes when these men of God wondered whether they truly were on the right track. Can't you imagine them asking, "God, where are *You* in all of this?"

Paul addresses these kinds of questions in his letter to the Colossians, where he tells us what the perfect will of God really looks like.

THE KNOWLEDGE OF GOD'S WILL

Paul told the Colossian Christians that he prayed unceasingly for them to "be *filled with the knowledge of His will* in all spiritual wisdom and understanding, so that you will walk in a manner worthy of the Lord, to please Him in all respects, bearing fruit in every good work and increasing in the knowledge of God" (Colossians 1:9–10, emphasis added).

The word *filled* here means totally and completely filled—no gaps, no holes, nothing left void. Does this mean that as a result of prayer we can have perfect understanding of God, His will, and everything He does? Of course not!

Rather, Paul tells us in Romans that we will not always grasp why His permissive will *allows* certain things to happen or why His sovereign will *decrees* that they will take place: "Oh, the depth of the riches both of the wisdom and knowledge of God! How unsearchable are His judgments and unfathomable His ways! For who has known the mind of the Lord, or who became His counselor?" (11:33–34).

Paul never tells us that God will fill us in on everything or that we will have a handle on why He does what He does. On the contrary, he asserts that we will never understand many things about God's sovereign will. Furthermore, our finite human minds aren't *capable* of fully understanding God's will. Therefore, Paul points out, God doesn't make everything perfectly clear to us—*even when it has to do specifically with us!*

In our democratic culture, that just doesn't seem

right, does it? It seems to many of us that since God is making decisions that may affect us directly, we have a right to know what He's up to. After all, shouldn't we have a say in what He does with us?

We need to remember that it's the Lord's prerogative to reveal or *not* to reveal to us certain things about His will. Why? Because He's God and we're not!

When Paul prays for the Colossians to be filled with the knowledge of God's will, he is actually praying that they will be *controlled* by it. In other words, while we may not have perfect knowledge of God's will, we are by faith to allow His will to control us and everything we do.

God's will, Paul says, is for us to seek to know Him better.

TO KNOW HIM AND LOVE HIM

As of the writing of this book, my wife and I are approaching our silver anniversary. We started out in the same kindergarten together, and now, after twenty-five years of marriage to Debbie, I'm more in love with her than ever. Like just about any couple, we've had things to work through, but I can tell you there has never been a moment when I've regretted marrying her. If I had it to do over, I'd marry her again!

You might think that a man who has been married to a woman he has been so truly, deeply, and madly in love with for almost a quarter-century would know all he wants to know about her. Not so with me and my Debbie! I have found that the more I find out about this wonderful person, the more I want to know—and sometimes *need* to know! I want to know more about how she thinks, how she feels, and what she wants from me.

I think this is what it means to be truly in love.

And I believe this should be the look of our love for God.

When Paul prayed for the Colossians to grow in their knowledge of God, he was not talking about mere head knowledge—knowing *about* God—but about a personal knowledge *of* Him. Paul said that it's important that those who know God personally continue to get to know Him better and better and love Him more and more.

Speaking through one of the Old Testament prophets, God said this about the importance of really *knowing* Him: "Thus says the LORD, 'Let not a wise man boast of his wisdom, and let not the mighty man boast of his might, let not a rich man boast of his riches; but let him who boasts boast of this, that he understands and knows Me" (Jeremiah 9:23–24).

God is telling us, "Don't brag about your degrees, about your salary, about your job position. I don't care about those things, and neither do the people around you. If you want to brag about anything, brag about how well you know Me."

Knowing God better and better—this is His will for us. And it's the only way He will lead us, guide us, and direct us in the way He wants us to go. We need an insatiable hunger to know God better, a hunger for more of Him. When we develop this hunger, the more we get to know God, and the more we'll want to know Him better.

Why do you suppose God wants us to have such a hunger to know Him? Is it because He's lonely and needs the company? Because He's vain and needs our approval? Hardly! God wants us to know Him better simply because He loves us and wants to bless us—with Himself. And when we make it our life's focus to know the Lord better, He gives us some incredible gifts, namely power, peace, and wisdom.

Knowing God Brings Spiritual Power

So many of us Christians are enslaved, not because we don't want to do what is right in the eyes of God and not because we don't *want* a growing Christian walk, but because we don't know the power available to us if we simply make knowing God our first priority.

The Bible tells us that God's people are destroyed for their lack of knowledge (see Hosea 4:6). We can see that all around us. People, even Bible-believing Christians, make foolish decisions, fall into sinful situations, and are enslaved by the Enemy, all because they lack a vital, growing knowledge of God.

On the other hand, the Bible promises us that a growing knowledge of God will give us power, even when we are faced with evil: "By smooth words he [the Antichrist] will turn to godlessness those who act wickedly toward the covenant, but *the people who know their God will display strength and take action*" (Daniel 11:32, emphasis added).

The key to knowing God's will is knowing Him, for when we focus on really knowing the Lord, He imparts His power to us.

Knowing God Brings Peace

For centuries, men and women of God have written and spoken about the peace of God and how it is part of God's perfect will for us. In his *Confessions,* the great pioneer of the faith Augustine of Hippo wrote this prayer: "Lord, thou madest us for thyself, and we can find no rest till we find rest in thee."

We find peace only in knowing God.

The apostle Peter, who knew Jesus as well as anyone, spoke of this kind of peace when he wrote, "Grace and peace be *multiplied* to you in the knowledge of God and of Jesus our Lord" (2 Peter 1:2, emphasis added). Peter received this promise of peace during a face-to-face encounter with Jesus, who told him and the rest of the apostles: "Peace I leave with you; My peace I give to you; not as the world gives do I give to you" (John 14:27).

The peace Peter received from Jesus and wrote about in his second epistle is a peace the world not only can't give but also doesn't understand. It doesn't depend on our circumstances, our financial situation, our relationship with our spouse, or our professional or social position. It surpasses all human comprehension (see Philippians 4:7).

Do you want that kind of peace? You will find it as you continue to get to know God in a deeper way. And it's His will that you do just that.

Knowing God Brings Wisdom

I want to tell you about two men I've had the opportunity to meet—I'll call them Ray and Bob.

Ray was a highly educated man. He spent years in college, seminary, and personal Bible study. He can tell you anything you want to know about the Bible and about doctrine. Bob, on the other hand, was self-educated. He had no formal degrees or training and only a basic knowledge of the Bible. If you had doctrinal questions, you wouldn't have gone to Bob for answers.

Ray seemingly knew all there is to learn about the Christian faith, but he couldn't seem to apply it consistently. Consequently, his life was a series of mistakes and bad decisions. Bob's life, on the other hand, radiated wisdom. He knew what God wanted from him, and he did it!

The difference between these two men? Bob had godly wisdom, while Ray had a head full of knowledge with little clue for applying it. Paul referred to Bob's kind of wisdom as a gift from God: "The Father of glory, may give to you a spirit of wisdom and of revelation in the knowledge of Him" (Ephesians 1:7).

The word *wisdom* here means collecting and organizing principles from Scripture in order to find guidance and direction. The word *understanding* means insight—the ability to assimilate facts and information in order to draw a right, godly conclusion. When you combine the wisdom and understanding Paul is talking about, you have the ability to take the Word of God, grasp the concepts and principles, and put them into practice in everyday life. This is known as application.

But there is a third aspect to this process. It's allowing God Himself to inscribe the wisdom and understanding into our hearts so that we can follow the guidance He gives us through His written Word. That is called *illumination.*

That is what the wisdom of God looks like in real life.

We can't acquire this kind of wisdom through any human means—through Bible college or seminary. We can't even get it through intensive Bible study. There is only one way to gain this kind of wisdom, and it's by allowing God the Father, through the work of the Holy Spirit, to impart His wisdom to us. And that happens as we get to know Him better.

When it comes to finding the will of God, there is no more comfortable place to be than in His very presence. And when we make it our life's focus to draw close to Him, we are drawn into a relationship in which we desire more than anything to worship Him.

When we do that, we are closer than ever to knowing His will for us.

WORSHIP AND THE WILL OF GOD

When we are frustrated in our attempts to know God's will for our lives, worshiping Him can move from its rightful place at the top of our list of priorities. But that's exactly the opposite of how it should be.

Paul suggests this in the first chapter of Colossians. In verse 9, Paul starts to pray for the Colossians' spiritual well-being. But beginning at verse 15, this prayer gives way to what theologians call a Christological hymn—a hymn sung in the ancient church. This hymn praises and worships the Lord for who He is:

Creator (vv. 15–16)

Sustainer (v. 17)

Head of the church (v. 18)

Redeemer (vv. 20, 22)

That's right! Paul went from praying for the Colossians straight to reciting a hymn of praise and worship.

This passage suggests two things. First, that worship is a basic, essential part of the Christian life. But it also suggests that it is not possible to determine God's will for our lives apart from worship—genuine worship from a heart that loves God.

When I hear people tell me that they feel directionless, as if God isn't leading and guiding them, one of the first questions I ask is, "How is your worship and praise life?" Often, the neglect of this vitally important part of our relationship leads us to feel as though God isn't giving us direction. Either we have completely overlooked worship and praise, or we are making one of the following mistakes:

1. *Giving God the leftovers.* See if this isn't a familiar picture. Mr. and Mrs. Christian work hard at their jobs

all week long and spend countless hours shuttling the kids to and from school, sports events, and church activities. In addition to all that, Mr. Christian goes to his men's club and to the golf course on weekends, and Mrs. Christian has her ladies' Bible studies, PTA meetings, and trips to the mall.

It's an exhausting schedule, and it leaves little time and energy for Mr. and Mrs. C to spend in personal prayer, worship, and praise. By the time Sunday morning rolls around, they barely have the energy to get out of bed and go to church. And once they are there, they mumble out the hymns and choruses as if they were funeral dirges, all the while thinking, *Let's get this over with so we can get home and rest.*

Sadly, this is an all-too-common picture of how we offer God the leftovers—leftover energy, leftover passion, leftover funds . . . leftover love.

If this is what our life of worship and praise looks like, is it any wonder we aren't sensing God's leading and guidance?

God spoke to His people very sternly of this practice of offering leftover worship: "A son honors his father, and a servant his master. Then if I am a father, where is My honor? And if I am a master, where is My respect? . . . You are presenting defiled food upon My altar. . . . Why not offer it to your governor? Would he be pleased with you? Or would he receive you kindly?" (Malachi 1:6–8).

Could you imagine throwing a dinner party for some important, high-profile people—perhaps high government officials—and offering them last night's leftovers? A menu of a half-consumed pot roast, day-old salad, bread barely on the good side of stale, and half a German chocolate cake for dessert? Of course not!

Neither should you think about offering God your leftover time and energy. All of these things are His to begin with, and you should offer Him only the best!

2. *Offering cheap worship.* Let's take that same dinner party but change the menu a little bit. Suppose that instead of serving leftovers, you invited all these VIPs to a nice hot meal . . . of TV dinners. Never mind that you'd announced a menu of prime rib, seasoned mashed potatoes, fresh vegetables, and an assortment of the most sumptuous pastries for dessert. Now these weren't just any TV dinners you served, but the best TV dinners money could buy. And you had a variety to choose from too! You even went so far as to put out a few extra cents to get the Thanksgiving-style turkey dinner with all the trimmings an aluminum tray could hold.

If you were to do that, I can assure you that your guests would be offended. They may not say anything on the spot, but that dinner party wouldn't do your reputation a bit of good.

No one in his or her right mind would go cheap like that at a dinner party with important guests. Neither should we go cheap when it comes to our worship of the Lord.

Again, some very strong words for those who go cheap when it comes to worship: "'Cursed be the swindler who has a male in his flock, and vows it, but sacrifices a blemished animal to the Lord, for I am a great King,' says the LORD of hosts" (Malachi 1:14). Cheap worship is not only unacceptable to God but offensive.

When we commit our hearts and lives to the Lord, we commit ourselves to giving Him our very best. Not out of a desire to pay Him back for what He's done for us—we could never repay Him in a million years—but out of gratitude for Him giving us *His* very best and out of deep love for Him.

If we want God to reveal His will for our lives, if we want His very best, then we should be willing to give Him our very best when it comes to worship. Not the leftovers and not some cheap substitute, but worship that comes from a heart of love, devotion, and gratitude for Him. When we do that, He is more than willing to reveal to us His will for our lives.

This brings us to a crucial part of seeking God's will: doing what He has already told us to do.

DON'T FORGET OBEDIENCE!

On April 10, 1912, the great ship *Titanic* embarked on its much-awaited maiden voyage from Southampton, England to New York. This ship was designed and constructed to be unsinkable. It was four massive city blocks long and equipped with the most up-to-date equipment and safety devices as well as plush dinning rooms and spacious staterooms. All of this was intended to allow the rich and the famous to sail the seas with confidence and in luxury.

However, the truth is that the ship was doomed

before she ever left port. She carried only half the lifeboats necessary for her passengers and crew. In spite of her carefully designed and constructed hull, which included various watertight chambers intended to keep the ship from sinking if one chamber became flooded, she sank within two hours and forty minutes after that fatal collision with an iceberg. Less time than it takes to watch the epic movie that shared her name.

Throughout the day of April 14, as the *Titanic* approached the iceberg that would sink her, she received no less than six communications warning her she was entering a dangerous field of ice. One message from the ship *Athinai* via the ship *Baltic* was posted five hours after it was received. The next was from the ship *Californian* to the ship *Antillian*. This message never made it to the captain because it would have interrupted his dinner. Another message from the ship *Mesaba* was never taken to the captain because the operator was by himself and could not leave his post. Then the final message, again from the *Californian*, was cut off in midtransmission because the ship's operator was carrying on his own conversation with commercial traffic. Even after that, the bridge received a warning from the *Rappahannock* by Morse lamp, but they never seemed to heed the warning.

In that sense, the *Titanic* was doomed for destruction before she ever left the port in Southampton.

That is exactly what happens when we disobey and ignore God's Word—the leading of the gentle voice of God. We are doomed at whatever we set out to do from the beginning. It is critical that we obey His commands.

That obedience is vital to those of us who want Him to reveal His will.

Paul wrote about the importance of obedience: "So that you will walk in a manner worthy of the Lord, to please Him in all respects, bearing fruit in every good work and increasing in the knowledge of God" (Colossians 1:10).

This verse says a lot about the connection between knowing God's will and obedience. This tells us that when we live in obedience to the direction God gives us through His Word, we can expect Him to give us further direction and guidance. But when we ignore that scriptural direction, put it off, or treat it nonchalantly, He will not reveal any further leading. In other words, what we do today with the direction He's already given to us determines how much direction He gives us for tomorrow.

We see this principle illustrated in the Christmas story in Matthew 2. Wise men called magi saw a star signaling the arrival of the Messiah, and they traveled to Bethlehem for one reason: "To worship Him" (v. 2). These men were familiar with the Old Testament prophecies concerning the coming of the Christ, and when they saw His star in the eastern sky, they knew what to do.

That was the only information they had concerning the birth of Jesus. And they acted on what they knew. The magi were faithful in following God's leading, and it was only because of that faithfulness that God allowed them to have such a special place in history.

The same is true for us today.

Instead of following God's general will for us, too many of us want to negotiate with Him or live as though the written Word doesn't apply to us individually. But God didn't give us the instructions recorded in a leather-bound book for us to negotiate or debate over. He gave us those instructions to obey!

This means simply surrendering ourselves to the will of God as we know it. We don't have to worry about how God wants us to live or what He's said yes or no to. It's all recorded for you specifically in the written, spoken Word of God.

Are you looking for a God who leads and guides you? You can find everything you need to know about Him within the pages of the best-selling book of all time, the Bible. And when you obey the instructions in that book—by making a commitment to get to know Him, to worship Him, and obey Him—you will have found the God who leads and guides you.

Reflections for
Individual or Small Group Study

1. How is the whole concept of God's will confused and misunderstood in our culture?

2. What do you believe is the basis for God's will and purpose for your life?

3. Why are purpose and direction so elusive for most people?

4. What role does the Bible play in leading and guiding our lives?

5. Do you believe you can find direction for every life decision in the Bible? Why? Why not?

6. In what ways does God speak to you and provide direction for your life?

THE GOD WHO HOLDS THE FUTURE

The future is something which everyone reaches at the rate of 60 minutes an hour, whatever he does, whoever he is.

■ C. S. LEWIS

NO ONE WILL FORGET where they were or what they were doing when the news broke, when one horrific chain of events shook our worlds to their very core.

On the morning of September 11, 2001, a day that will live on in the minds and hearts of Americans and others around the world for generations to come, a handful of religious extremists—armed with nothing more than some box cutters and a seething hatred for the United States—hijacked four commercial airliners and threw our world into chaos. In a matter of minutes, thousands of people lost their lives, many thousands more lost their livelihoods, and all of us lost our sense of invulnerability as two of the jets slammed into the twin towers of the World Trade Center, the symbol of American wealth and prosperity, and another hit the Pentagon, the symbol of American military superiority.

No one knows for sure where the fourth hijacked airliner was headed or what further devastation it might have caused. Was it headed for the White House? Capitol Hill? It was only because of the heroic actions of some of the passengers and crew of Flight 93, led by a godly man named Todd Beamer, that we didn't find out.

As it was, the events of that one horrible morning cost more than three thousand lives, and it cost the American economy—already in recession at the time—an estimated $120 billion dollars. As of this writing, the effects of those losses are still being felt in many sectors of our economy.

Even more devastating than the economic costs of September 11 is the immeasurable effect it has had on the psyche of the American people. We all had the horrible images—of those magnificent towers burning and then collapsing, of people jumping from the towers' windows to their deaths, of terrified men and women running from the scene, of dust and rubble littering the streets of Manhattan—seared into our minds forever. Since that day, poll after poll suggests that we don't feel physically safe and secure, that we see our way of life in peril, and that we see our nation as vulnerable to another attack at least as damaging and deadly as the ones that took place that morning. Many people believe it's not a matter of *if* we are attacked again but *when*—and with even more devastating results.

In the days, weeks, and months following the attacks, the fear and anxiety in our nation was palpable. Government institutions of all levels and news organizations around the world heard rumors and threats of further attacks, of "the other shoe dropping." Since that time, we have received numerous threats—many of them considered credible—concerning further attacks, some reportedly coming directly from the mouth of terrorist mastermind Osama bin Laden himself.

We all heard the questions from people who didn't know what to make of what they had just witnessed:

"Where is God in all of this?"

"Is this a part of the end-times prophecies?"

"Is this God's judgment on the United States?"

"What's going to happen next?"

"Is this the beginning of the end of the world?"

I believe all these questions can be summed up in the one question we all desperately need answered: "Is God really in control?"

Now more than ever, I believe that people are looking for a God who holds the future, who has under control a world that seems to be spinning into chaos. We long to know with certainty that even in a time of frightening world events—with wars and rumors of wars, acts of terrorism and hatred, economic uncertainty, and one international crisis after another making headlines on a daily basis—God has things in hand.

More than that, I believe people are looking for a

God who not only controls this world and where it is headed but who also guides and directs our personal futures.

I want you to know that we serve a loving God, and that no matter what world events may unfold before us, He is firmly in control.

THE LORD WILL HAVE THE FINAL SAY

While we may wonder and worry over our futures and the future of our world, God does not. You see, God has never been and never will be held captive by any human or natural event. Nothing takes God by surprise or overwhelms or dumbfounds Him. That's because God holds the future of all nations and all people in the palm of His hand.

The psalmist reveals, in a conversation between the Father and the Son, that God not only controls our world and what happens in it—He owns every square inch of it: "Ask of Me, and I will surely give the nations as Your inheritance, And the very ends of the earth as Your possession" (Psalm 2:8).

IN THE MIDST OF CHAOS, HE'S IN CONTROL

Speaking through the Old Testament prophet Ezekiel, the Lord assures us that He alone controls the future and world events. In chapters 38–39, Ezekiel paints a fairly frightening picture of coming war, death, and suffering. But this passage also communicates a message we all need to hear today: "No matter what happens, I am still the Lord, and nothing will take place outside of My perfect will for the people I love."

In Ezekiel 38, the Lord warns us that one day a coalition of ten military powers will unite in an attempt to destroy God's chosen nation, Israel:

> "Son of man, set your face toward Gog of the land of Magog, the prince of Rosh, Meshech, and Tubal, and prophesy against him, and say, 'Thus says the Lord GOD, "Behold, I am against you, O Gog, prince of Rosh, Meshech, and Tubal. And I will turn you about, and put hooks into your jaws, and I will bring you out, and all your army, horses and horsemen, all of them splendidly attired, a great company with buckler and shield, all of them wielding swords; Persia, Ethiopia, and Put with them, all of them with shield and helmet; Gomer with all its troops; Beth-togarmah from the remote parts of the north with all its troops—many peoples with you." ' " (Ezekiel 38:2–6)

Oceans of ink and reams of paper have been used in writing speculations about Gog and Magog. I'm not certain what I believe about who or what Gog is. Most scholars understand it to be not a geographical location but a title—such as a chief, prince, or any other title symbolic of national or military leadership. Evidently, Gog is the general, or leader, over a coalition of forces or countries mentioned here.

Magog is understood to be the land or lands of nations or powers. But who are they? First-century Jewish historian Flavius Josephus, considered in many quarters to be the greatest historian of all time, asserted that "Magogians" were the same people the Greeks of that time called the Scythians—a nomadic people who lived in and came out of central Asia into parts of what was, until recently, the Soviet Union. Their descendants occupy former Soviet republics such as Kazakhstan, Kirghizia, Uzbekistan, Turkmenistan, Tajikistan, and the Ukraine.

There are any number of interpretations of this passage and who exactly the nations or powers joining Gog and Magog will be. Some of them are easily identifiable. We know that Put is modern-day Libya, Persia is modern-day Iran, and biblical Ethiopia includes part of that country as well as northern Sudan and part of Somalia. We can identify Beth-togarmah as what is known today as Turkey, and scholars tell that Meshech, Tubal, and Gomer are also linked to that nation.

The identities of the other nations listed in this text are open to conjecture at this time in history. In fact, the guesses and theories as to who some of these powers are have changed as the political map of the world has changed.

For example, through the centuries—and particularly during the Cold War period, when the Soviet Union was a real and present threat—Rosh was thought by many to be Russia. I believe this is a faulty reading of that text. The best scholars now tell us that the word *Rosh* refers to the ancient people known as the Sarmatians, who lived in that area north of Iran, Iraq, and Turkey, around the Caspian and Black Seas.

What is quite chilling—even frightening for those who don't realize that our God is in control of the situation—is that with the exception of the Ukraine, all of the nations I've identified here are committed Islamic states. And many of them are radically Islamic, meaning that they have an intense hatred for both Israel and for the United States. Some of these nations are now taking part in systematic persecution of Jews and Christians. For example, in the Sudan, radical Muslims have taken to crucifying Christians. Even worse, some of these nation states reportedly have nuclear weapons left over from the old Soviet Union.

The stated goal of many radical Muslim leaders is the destruction of the state of Israel. They believe Islam teaches that because of the disobedience of the Jewish people, the Muslims replaced them as God's chosen people. For that reason, the reestablishment of the Jewish state in what we know as the Promised Land, which radical Muslims see as their own, contradicts how they see the teachings of Mohammed. They believe that allowing the Jewish people to occupy the Holy Land makes Mohammed a false prophet, and they further believe that the Koran teaches that they must defeat and kill the "infidels"—Jews and Christians.

When you put all this information together, it isn't hard to imagine a time—and one not far off—when these nations could make their move to attempt to eradicate Israel, as well as the United States, from the world map.

While we can't be certain of who some of these military powers are, we can be sure of one thing: There will come a day when they will unite against Israel and try to destroy her. Ezekiel 38:10 tells us that they will devise an evil plan, but we can see that it is God, and not these powers, who is in control. In verse 4 of that same chapter, we are told that God will put hooks in his jaws and will bring him down and then in. It's almost as though these powers have no choice in the matter, as though they are being *drawn* into the conflict.

Before I go on here, I want to pose some questions.

Does God hate the Islamic nations? Does He hate Muslims? No! God said in His Word that He is not willing that any would enter eternity without receiving His gift of eternal life through Christ Jesus (see 2 Peter 3:9). The Lord longs that every Muslim would know not Mohammed but God's one and only Son, the true Messiah, Jesus Christ. And He tells us that out of what is now the Islamic world, throngs of people will give their lives to Him.

King David, in one of his prophetic psalms, tells us, "Envoys will come out of Egypt; Ethiopia will quickly stretch out her hands to God" (Psalm 68:31). The prophet Isaiah also wrote, "In that day there will be an altar to the LORD in the midst of the land of Egypt . . . and the Egyptians will worship with the Assyrians . . . whom the LORD of hosts has blessed, saying, 'Blessed is Egypt My people, and Assyria the work of My hands, and Israel My inheritance'" (Isaiah 19:19, 23, 25).

This tells us two things. First, God will have the

last say over the Islamic nations. Second, it tells us
that no matter how violent or bloody things may get,
He will still be reaching out to bring these people to
Himself. This means that out of these nations—
including the ones who will rise up against Israel—
will come those who will turn to the true and living
God and worship Him. In fact, God goes so far as to call
these people "blessed"—the same thing He calls Israel.

The apostle John wrote of the final result of this
outpouring of God's Spirit on all people, including
the Islamic peoples: "A great multitude, which no one
could count, *from every nation and all tribes and peoples
and tongues,* standing before the throne and before
the Lamb . . . cry out with a loud voice, saying, 'Salvation to our God who sits on the throne, and to the
Lamb'" (Revelation 7:9–10, emphasis added).

That is a picture of a God who is firmly in control
of all of humanity. And it's a picture of a God who has
His hand of protection over His chosen people.

GOD'S CONTROL OVER ISRAEL'S DESTINY

The nation of Israel has an eye in the sky, and that's
not a satellite. God has promised that He will keep a
24-7 watch over His chosen people. The psalmist wrote,
"Behold, He who keeps Israel Will neither slumber nor
sleep" (Psalm 121:4). And the prophet Daniel wrote of
an archangel standing guard over the Jewish people:
"Now at that time Michael, the great prince who stands
guard over the sons of your people . . . " (Daniel 12:1).

God tells us that when the confederation of military

powers under Gog and Magog moves against Jerusalem, the Lord will intervene in spectacular fashion:
"'It will come about on that day, when Gog comes
against the land of Israel,' declares the Lord God, 'that
My fury will mount up in My anger'" (Ezekiel 38:18).

The wording in this verse can be read to literally
mean that God will be coming down breathing fire
over what is going on. In other words, He is absolutely furious! And why? Another of the Old Testament prophetic books says it this way: "For thus says
the LORD of hosts, '. . . He has sent me against the
nations which plunder you, for he who touches you,
touches the apple of His eye'" (Zechariah 2:8).

When God uses the phrase *apple of His eye*, He is
referring to His own chosen people—the Jews. God
tells us that even though the people of Israel have
fallen away from their faith in God and have rejected
the Messiah, He still holds a special love for them.
Not only that, He tells us in His word that attacking
Israel is the equivalent of attacking Him personally.

This scene of battle will not be a pleasant place
when God brings His intervention. Ezekiel wrote of a
devastating earthquake hitting the area (38:19), of
mass confusion within the ranks of Gog's confederation (v. 21), and of fire-and-brimstone judgment
pouring down on those who come against Israel
(v. 22). Ezekiel includes in this story a horrible account of casualties so staggering that the Israelis will
burn the leftover implements of war for seven years,
and it will take them seven months to bury the dead
just so the land can be purified (39:9–12).

From the human standpoint, things look very bleak. This is a dreadful picture of destruction and death that most of us can't even comprehend. It looks like the combination of an all-out nuclear attack combined with every natural disaster we've ever heard of—all rolled into one event.

But in this same passage, God tells us that this world is not going to spin out of His control. In the midst of all this, He has a plan.

EZEKIEL'S BLESSED MESSAGE: OUR GOD HOLDS THE FUTURE!

As horrible as the scene described in Ezekiel 38–39 is, the Lord tells us that all these things will take place for a purpose: His purpose! It is through all the wickedness of godless people and nations that He will be glorified.

That sounds like a real paradox, doesn't it? How can God glorify Himself in the midst of all this violence, death, and hatred? That happens, He tells us, because no matter what kind of actions people take, no matter what decisions they make, He will take the worst events and turn them around for the glory and furtherance of His kingdom.

All through Ezekiel 38–39, this message is repeated like a chorus:

"in order that the nations may know Me" (38:16)
"I shall magnify Myself . . . and make Myself known" (v. 23)

"They will know that I am the Lord" (39:6)
"My holy name I shall make known . . . and I shall not let My holy name be profaned anymore" (39:7)
"And I shall set My glory among the nations; and all the nations will see My judgment which I have executed" (39:21)

In short, it will become clear to everyone that God is God and that He alone is in control. As Paul wrote, "At the name of Jesus every knee will bow, of those who are in heaven, and on earth, and under the earth, and that every tongue will confess that Jesus Christ is Lord, to the glory of God the Father" (Philippians 2:10–11).

As much as they hate the Jewish people and want them wiped from the face of the earth, Yasser Arafat, Saddam Hussein, Osama bin Laden, and others like them won't have the last word on Israel. Neither will one of her truest, most devoted friends, the United States. The Jews are God's chosen people, and He will have the final say over their destiny.

Not only that, God is firmly in control of the future of all of humankind and of this world. That includes your future and mine.

OUR FUTURES ARE IN HIS HANDS

There is a line of theology—a quite wrong line, I must add—that holds a view of God as the One who created the cosmos, the Earth, and all its inhabitants, but who now stands back and lets events occur as they will. This belief system essentially holds that all things occur in line with the natural laws God has set up, with some human influences and no kind of additional divine intervention. Paul described people who hold to this kind of theology as "holding to a form of godliness, although they have denied its power" (2 Timothy 3:5).

This line of thinking is called *deism,* and it's a far cry from the picture of God I've written about in this book. I believe in a God who has saved me, loves me, provides for me, and holds and guides my own personal future. And since I love and serve this God, I can rest in Him, free of fear and anxiety for the future.

In the Sermon on the Mount, Jesus assured multitudes of listeners that those who put their faith in God needn't worry about the future: "Seek first His kingdom and His righteousness, and all these things will be added to you. So do not worry about tomorrow; for tomorrow will care for itself" (Matthew 6:33–34).

Sadly, this is not a picture of Christianity in our nation today.

We American Christians live in a time of great spiritual malaise. We are a religious people, but the joy of knowing God, of loving and serving Him, has gone out of many of our lives and has been replaced with a sense of despondency, feebleness, and depression. We have drifted into a spiritual darkness that has left us feeling helpless, hopeless, and fearful about the future. It's as if the light that Christ put within us has either been snuffed out or has been so obscured that the world can't see it.

I believe this has happened because we American Christians are more concerned with our affluence and wealth, comfort and position—the things we saw viciously attacked on September 11, 2001—than we are about our spiritual condition.

We in America are in great need of personal spiritual revival. And that will happen only when we place our faith in a God who knows and controls the future, when we believe the promise He spoke through the prophet Jeremiah: "'For I know the plans that I have for you,' declares the LORD, 'plans for welfare and not for calamity to give you a future and a hope'" (Jeremiah 29:11).

We can rest assured that we have a God who loves us, who guides and directs us, who forgives us, and has made a way for us to live in paradise with Him for all of eternity. And He's also the God who has the events of this world—and the things that take place in our own lives—firmly under control.

He is a God we can rest in and trust to care for us not only in this life but also in the eternal life to come, if we but put our trust in the work of His Son, the Lord Jesus Christ.

He is the God we are all searching for!

REFLECTIONS FOR
INDIVIDUAL OR SMALL GROUP STUDY

1. In what way did the events of September 11, 2001 become a watershed experience for America?

2. Why and how do such traumatic events cause us to fear and become anxious?

3. How have Christians responded to the spiritual questions the world began asking post-9-11?

4. How does having a clear and faith-filled perspective on the future help in times of uncertainty?

5. Why do you think God would choose to allow tragedy in our lives?

6. What difference does really knowing Him through Jesus make in your daily life?

NOTES

Chapter 1: Searching for the Sacred
1. "Religious Transcendence or Midlife Crisis?" *Psychology Today* 26 (September/October 1993): 46.

Chapter 3: The Bridge God Built
1. Steven J. Lawson, *Made in Our Image: What Shall We Do with a "User-Friendly" God?* (Sisters, Ore.: Multnomah Publishers, 2000), 44.

SINCE 1894, Moody Publishers has been dedicated to equip and motivate people to advance the cause of Christ by publishing evangelical Christian literature and other media for all ages around the world. Because we are a ministry of the Moody Bible Institute of Chicago, a portion of the proceeds from the sale of this book go to train the next generation of Christian leaders.

If we may serve you in any way in your spiritual journey toward understanding Christ and the Christian life, please contact us at www.moodypublishers.com.

"All Scripture is God-breathed and is useful for teaching, rebuking, correcting and training in righteousness, so that the man of God may be thoroughly equipped for every good work."
—2 TIMOTHY 3:16, 17

MOODY
PUBLISHERS

THE NAME YOU CAN TRUST®

The God You've Been Searching For Team

Acquiring Editor:
Mark Tobey

Copy Editor:
Wendy Peterson

Back Cover Copy:
Lisa Cockrel

Cover Design:
Paetzold Design

Interior Design:
Ragont Design

Printing and Binding:
Versa Press, Inc.

The typeface for the text of this book is
Giovanni